BATTLESHIPS OF THE
BISMARCK CLASS

BATTLESHIPS OF THE
BISMARCK CLASS

Bismarck and *Tirpitz*: Culmination and
Finale of German Battleship Construction

Gerhard Koop and Klaus-Peter Schmolke

Translated from the German by Geoffrey Brooks

GREENHILL BOOKS, LONDON
NAVAL INSTITUTE PRESS, ANNAPOLIS, MARYLAND

Battleships of the Bismarck Class
First published 1998 by Greenhill Books, Lionel Leventhal
Limited, Park House, 1 Russell Gardens, London NW11 9NN

Published and distributed in the United States of America by the
Naval Institute Press, 118 Maryland Avenue, Annapolis,
Maryland 21402-5035

© Bernard & Graefe Verlag, Koblenz, 1990
English language edition © Lionel Leventhal Limited, 1998

British Library Cataloguing in Publication Data
Koop, Gerhard
Battleships of the Bismarck class:the Bismarck and Tirpitz:
culmination and finale of German battleship construction
1. Battleships – Germany – History 2. World War, 1939–1945 –
Naval operations, German
I. Title II. Schmolke, Klaus-Peter
623.8'252'0943'09044

Greenhill ISBN 1-85367-320-X

Library of Congress Catalog Card Number 97-76483

Naval Institute Press ISBN 1-55750-049-5

Publishing History
Battleships of the Bismarck Class is translated from *Die
Schlachtschiffe der Bismarck-Klasse* first published by Bernard
& Graefe Verlag, Koblenz, 1990.

Printed and bound in Singapore by Kyodo Printing Company

Contents

Photographs

Line Illustrations

Foreword

This first volume of a new series entitled 'Ship Classes of the German Navy' is devoted to the two battleships of the *Bismarck* class, *Bismarck* and *Tirpitz*, the largest capital ships ever built and completed in Germany.

Bismarck and *Tirpitz* were simultaneously the culmination and finale of a German capital ship building industry which—at least, as seen from a modern view of the basic strategic considerations—was misdirected. Both units enjoyed only a brief existence; and though begun during peacetime, both were commissioned after the outbreak of the Second World War. *Bismarck*'s fate embraced triumph and tragedy; and over a limited period *Tirpitz* could do no more than prove her value simply by her existence—and this, for a warship of these dimensions, was probably too little. Skulking deep in Norwegian fjords, *Tirpitz* met her end suddenly, being destroyed by a combination of aerial bombing and inadequate underwater surveying. Addressing the Fleet after the destruction of *Bismarck* at the end of her first and last operation, the Commander of the Home Fleet, Admiral Sir John Tovey, said, 'The *Bismarck* put up a most gallant fight against impossible odds, worthy of the old days of the Imperial German Navy, and she went down with her flag flying.'

This *Bismarck* class volume lays the foundation for a series depicting various classes of German Navy heavy ships. The books will appear successively at intervals. The focus is pictorial and technical, the latter aspect concentrating on the rendering of technical principles, informative constructional plans and detailed sketches to a high standard. In selecting the illustrations, the primary aim has been to use previously unpublished photographs, where possible from private collections, taking into account what has already appeared in other publications so as to avoid repetition.

The books of this series, which feature each unit of a particular class, are complemented by parallel volumes of the series *Vom Original zum Modell* and *Planrolle* currently in preparation. It is proposed that this latter 'documentation in picture and plan' will be restricted to the name-ship of the class only; however, as insufficient source material was available for *Bismarck*, *Tirpitz* has been substituted as an exception to the rule.

Vom Original zum Modell in particular completes the technical presentation by supplying further detailed photographs of constructional stages and weapons which, together with the comprehensive line drawings, provide a high-quality source of information for anyone who is interested in the technology of battleships, not least the model builder. An interesting pictorial survey about models of the ships dealt with in the series is also being prepared. In *The Battleships of the Bismarck Class*, the plans material, though complete, could only be presented in miniature.

My thanks are due first of all to Klaus-Peter Schmolke, who prepared all plans and sketches in completed form. Next I thank *Fregattenkapitän* (retired) A. Schmolke, who served aboard *Tirpitz* from October 1940 to August 1942 as Senior Electrical ERA, and critically reviewed the manuscript. Thanks must also be extended to *Herr* F. Bavendamm, who gave me technical support in the choice and reproduction of photographs. Last but not least, I owe my thanks to my original publishers, Bernard & Graefe Verlag, for the confidence they gave me to pursue this project. Further information and suggestions from readers are always welcome.

All plans and sketches were prepared by Klaus-Peter Schmolke. Sources of photographs were Kriegsmarinewerft Wilhelmshaven (24), Royal Navy/Royal Air Force (18), PK/Koop Collection/Gally (118); Dünnhaupt (3), Schwettmann (9), AP (1), Klein (3) and Schmolke (11).

Gerhard Koop

Development and Construction

The signing of the Anglo-German Naval Agreement on 18 June 1936 paved the way for the construction by Germany of genuine capital ships which, from their conception, were similar in terms of their dimensions and armament to foreign units of the type.

Until then, Germany had been forbidden to build warships in excess of 10,000 tons displacement. The three *Panzerschiffe* (armoured ships) of the *Deutschland* class were around this limit: the battleships *Scharnhorst* and *Gneisenau*, built a little later and originally conceived as *Panzerschiffe*, represented an intermediate stage in battleship construction and were substantially in excess of the permitted tonnage. However, although they had been built in contravention of the treaties in force at the time, the 1935 Naval Agreement sanctioned their construction retroactively. That this particular Naval Agreement came into existence at all was the outcome of a voluntary offer by the Reich to limit the size of the German Fleet to a specific percentage of that of the Royal Navy, thereby dispelling fears that it might be the purpose of a future German Fleet to challenge British naval supremacy.

For Germany, at least with regard to the nature of the ships she was allowed to have, the Agreement signified the lifting of all the prohibitions and restrictions respecting German naval forces which had been imposed by the Treaty of Versailles, signed on 28 June 1919 and in force since 10 January 1920. But, as the French were to observe, the 'guilt' for this enormous and 'highly official' abrogation of part of the Versailles Treaty lay with Great Britain. The Agreement of 18 June 1935 tends to be conveniently forgotten in historical perspectives contemplating the unilateral infringements of the Versailles Treaty by Germany.

As respects the size and armament of the ship types embraced by the Agreement, other treaties which had been signed by the major sea powers in the interim were the following:

● The Washington Treaty of 6 February 1922 signed by the five major powers—the United States, Great Britain, Japan, France and Italy—placed limits on naval armaments. It laid down for the individual maritime powers, *inter alia*, the total tonnage for battleships and cruisers, together with the number of units the navies were permitted to have of each type, their size and armament and so on. Furthermore, it provided for the scrapping of many capital ships and (with some exceptions) imposed a ten-year moratorium on new construction. An upper limit of 35,000 tons and a maximum gun calibre of 38.1cm (16in) was set for future capital ship building. The limitation of ship size led to the introduction for the first time of a legal definition of displacement:

'. . . Standard displacement is the displacement of the vessel complete, fully manned, equipped with all machinery and ready for sea, including ammunition, equipment, provisions, food and fresh water for her crew, and miscellaneous stores and implements of every description to be carried in war, but not including fuel or reserve feedwater.'

● The London Naval Conference of 22 April 1930, in which the Washington Agreement was confirmed and extended by far-reaching regulations concerning the size and armament of cruisers and destroyers, was signed by the United States, Great Britain and Japan.

● The Anglo-German Agreement of 1935 was followed on 25 March 1936 by a further London Agreement, in which the standard displacement was redefined, and particular types of ship, their weapons and size were re-specified. This treaty was not signed by Italy or Japan, both of which had been exploring other avenues for some time, and even the United States took only a half-hearted interest. The new displacement clause stipulated that

'. . . The standard displacement of a surface vessel is the displacement of the completed ship, fully manned, provided with all machinery and ready to put to sea, including all armaments, ammunition, equipment and installations, supplies of food and fresh water for her crew together with supplies and instruments of every description which would be carried in war, but without fuel and reserve boiler water.'

In pursuance of rights now imbued by treaty, the German Navy was practically treading new ground with the construction of the two planned battleships, 'F' *Ersatz Hannover* (later *Bismarck*) and 'G' *Ersatz Schleswig-Holstein* (later *Tirpitz*), for it had been about twenty years since capital ships had last been built for the German Fleet.[1]

The most recent new construction in German yards had been:

● *Kriegsmarine Werft, Wilhelmshaven*
Battleship *König* (launched 1913)
Battlecruiser *Hindenburg* (launched 1915)
Battlecruiser *Ersatz* 'A' (begun 1915 but never completed)

● *Blohm & Voss, Hamburg*
Battlecruiser *Derfflinger* (launched 1913)
Battlecruiser *Mackensen* (begun 1914 but never completed)
Heavy cruiser *Prinz Eitel Friedrich* (begun 1915 but never completed)
Heavy cruiser *Ersatz Scharnhorst* (begun 1916 but never completed)

Each of these two yards would receive a contract to build one of the new units. At the time, they were the only German shipyards which were in a position to accept orders for ships of this type and size (the Deutsche Werke, Kiel, which had been developed from the Kaiserliche Werft in 1919, had full order books for other vessels, as was the case with other major German shipyards).

The sketch design was produced by the Construction Office in 1933 and the final design agreed in 1936. The plans were frequently amended by adjustments, additions and deletions during building. The official responsible for the project at the Naval Construction Office was ministerial adviser Hermann Burckhardt, who later supervised the launching of *Tirpitz*.

The ships' construction was based on the system of transverse and longitudinal frames proven in practice by the Imperial Navy. The hulls were divided into 22 watertight compartments (I–XXII) and welded to approximately 90 per cent. The double bottom covered about 83 per cent of the ships' length. The stems had a small bulge at the forefoot, and the bottoms had four bilge keels fitted. The basic design had been oriented towards compliance with the 35,000-ton limit for standard displacement.

The final 1936 design provided for another pair of catapults for aircraft situated forward and aft between the funnel and the after command centre, but in the light of British experience this was altered in 1938, when changes to the forward bridge and upper deck superstructure were also introduced.

Although both ships were of the same type and class, there were substantial differences between them. Whilst *Bismarck*'s funnel cap was silver-grey, that on *Tirpitz* was always black. The two cranes on *Bismarck* were sited 3m further aft and 3.5m further outboard than on her sister, and *Tirpitz* mounted these on the superstructure deck.

On *Bismarck*, the 10.5cm flak guns (starboard II and port II) were installed 5m further inboard. At the time of launching, *Bismarck*'s stem was straight while *Tirpitz* had the 'Atlantic bow'. Prior to commissioning, both ships were fitted with a degaussing coil at the lower edge of the armour at the designed waterline.

During the course of her service, *Tirpitz* received a number of modifications. To augment the increased battery of single 2cm guns, additional 2cm quadruple flak mountings were installed, for example on 'B' turret and atop the bridge structure: by 1944 she had 18 of these quadruples, mounted nine each side. The large searchlights under their anti-splinter guards on the funnel platform were removed to make way for further flak guns.

Bismarck was equipped with a single hangar on either side of the funnel and a double hangar at the foot

---

[1] 'F' and 'G' are identification letters for new warships under construction. A capital letter indicates a capital ship, a lower case letter a cruiser. A letter standing alone indicates an addition to the fleet, while a letter plus *'Ersatz'* (replacement) is a new ship to replace an existing unit.

of the mainmast, enabling her to carry six aircraft if needed (although in fact no more than four were ever shipped). On *Tirpitz* there were two hangars for two aircraft each at the base of the mainmast: if six aircraft had been required, two could have been carried, one on each catapult, in the open. The upper portion of the mainmast could be retracted telescopically.

Below: The launching ceremony for *Bismarck* at the Blohm & Voss yard, Hamburg.

Bismarck class: Technical Layout

GENERAL DETAILS

	Bismarck	*Tirpitz*
Building costs	196.m RM	191.6m RM
Measurement (gross or net registered tons)	28,181grt	28,160grt
	11,110nrt	
Official displacement	35,000 tons	35,000 tons
Actual displacement	(August 1940)	(February 1941)
empty	39,517 tonnes	39,539 tonnes
designed	45,451 tonnes	45,474 tonnes
full	49,406 tonnes	49,429 tonnes
maximum	50,405 tonnes	50,425 tonnes
		(53,500 tonnes 1944)
LOA	250.5m	253.6m
LWL	241.55m	241.72m
Beam	36m	36m
Maximum draught	10.2m	10.61m
	(at 49,406 tonnes)	(at 52,890 tonnes)
Designed draught	9.3m	9.9m
Height of sides (measured from keel top edge)	15m	15m
Machinery output designed	138,000shp	138,000shp
maximum	150,170shp	163,026shp
at		
Shaft revolutions designed	250/min	250/min
maximum	278/min	278/min
Speed designed	28kt	29kt
maximum	30.8kt	30.8kt
Range	8,525nm at 19kt	8,870nm at 19kt
	9,280nm at 16kt	
Bunkers designed	3,200m^3	3,200m^3
maximum	7,400m^3	7,780m^3
Ship's company	103 officers, 1,962 + 27 men (1941)	108 officers, 2,500 men (1943)
Watertight compartments	XXII	XXII
Immersion per cm	+57.3 tonnes	
Uniform trim moment	66,904m^4	
One double catapult	4 × Arado 196 aircraft	4 × Arado 196 aircraft
Searchlights, triaxially stabilised and directed centrally (those positioned on Tirpitz's funnel platform later replaced by flak)	7	7
Cranes	2	2
Ship's boats	3 barges, 4 picket boats, 1 launch, 2 cutters, 2 dinghies, 2 yawls (*Tirpitz* later probably fewer)	
Anchors	3 bow, 1 stern	

DESIGN AND CONSTRUCTION DETAILS (after Witte, as at 1936/38)

Length, cwl (construction waterline)		241.5m	241.5m
Beam, cwl		36m	36m
Height of side, measured from upper side, keel		15m	15
Freeboard, amidships		5.67m	5.67m
Freeboard, bow		8.8m	8.8m
Construction draught		9.33m	9.33m
Construction shaft output, maximum unforced		111,000shp	111,000shp
Construction speed, maximum unforced		31.5kt	31.5kt
Crew		2,200	2,200
Building steel		ST 52	ST 52
Main armament		8 × 38 cm	8 × 38 cm
Secondary armament (excluding MGs)		12 × 15 cm	12 × 15 cm
		14 × 10.5 cm	14 × 10.5 cm
Torpedo battery		Nil	Nil
Aircraft		4	4
Armour thickness	(deck) max.	110mm approx.	110mm approx.
	(side) max.	380mm approx.	380mm approx.
Range at cruising speed		9,250nm approx. at 19kt	9,250nm approx. at 19kt

Coefficients of Form at a Displacement of 45,951 tonnes

Ratio length cwl/beam	6.71	6.71
Ratio beam/draught	3.85	3.85
Longitudinal prismatic coefficient (δ)[1]	0.55	0.55
Coefficient, fineness of waterplane (α)[2]	0.66	0.66
Ratio δ/α	0.83	0.83
Midship section coefficient (β)[3]	0.97	0.97
Ratio δ/β	0.57	0.57

Weight Grouping

Individual construction groups have an identification letter used initially for calculation purposes in the design stages but ultimately retained throughout the period of the ship's useful life.

S = Weight of compartmented hull, comprising SI (building materials, e.g. steel ST 45 and ST 52, excluding waterline armour), S II (metalworkers), S III (carpenters), S IV (painters).

MI = Main machinery and connections, condensers, gears, couplings, shaft connections, propellers, auxiliary machinery, conduits and piping used in connection with the operation of the main machinery, exhaust/funnel cap, equipment etc., boilers with armatures, oil and water in the main engine plant.

---

[1]The longitudinal prismatic coefficient is the ratio of the volume of displacement to the volume of a prism having a length equal to the length between perpendiculars and a cross-sectional area equal to the midship sectional area.

[2]The fineness of waterplane coefficient is the ratio of the area of the waterplane to the area of its circumscribing rectangle.

[3]The midship section coefficient is the ratio of the midship section area to the area of a rectangle whose sides are equal to the draught and breadth extreme amidships.

MII = Auxiliary boiler plant, ship's heating system, washing and drinking water desalination plant, laundry, ablutions, kitchen gear etc., ship's pumps, primary electrical plant, lighting, cables, steering assembly, capstans, boats' windlasses, room fans, weapon systems, refrigerating plant, searchlights, signal lamps, command elements, gyro compass, mileage logs, sirens and workshops.

The remaining groups are indicated by the appropriate identification letter below.

All weights are expressed hereunder in metric tonnes.

Ship (SI–SIV), including armour and ship's gear, consumables, crew, effects, provisions and fresh water (details for *Bismarck* from Gröner)	11,691t	11,691t
Armour less turrets	17,450t	17,450t
Main machinery plant with equipment (MI)	2,800t	2,800t
Fuel, lubricating oil, boiler feedwater	7,216t	
Auxiliary machinery with equipment (MII)	1,428t	1,428t
(A) Armament and equipment (plus ammunition)	(Plus artillery armour)	5,973t (7,577t)
(T) Torpedo system	Nil	Nil
(F) Aircraft installation	83t	80t
(Spr) Defensive weapons	8t	8t
(I) General equipment	369.4t	361t
(N) Nautical equipment	8.6t	9t
(T) Masts and rigging	30t	30t
Empty ship with equipment	39,931.2t	39,931t
Ammunition	1,510.4t	1,510t
Torpedoes	Nil	Nil
Defensive equipment	2.5t	3t
Aircraft ammunition	Nil	Nil
Consumables	155.4t	156t
Crew and effects	243.6t	247t
Provisions	194.2t	194t
Type displacement (without drinking and washing water)	42,343.5t	42,077t
Drinking water	139.2t	139t
Washing water	167t	167t
Boiler feedwater	187.5t (battle cells)	188t
Fuel oil	3,226t	3,226t
Diesel fuel oil	96.5t	94t
Lubricating oil	80t	80t
Aviation spirit and coolant	17t (one filling)	17t
Construction displacement	45,950.5t	45,951t
Supplementaries:		
Boiler feedwater	187.5t	188t
Fuel oil	3,226t	3,226t
Diesel fuel oil	96.5t	97t
Lubricating oil	80t	80t
Aviation spirit and coolant	17t	17t

Reserve fresh water	389.2t	389t
Full displacement	49,946.7t	49,948t

(*Bismarck* special supplement fuel 1,009t; actual full displacement 50,955.7t)

Weights (rounded off and in percentages per Halder)

Ship's hull	12,700t	27.0%
Engine plant	3,000t	6.4%
Fuel/coolant installations	1,400t	3.0%
Armament	5,500t	11.8%
Armour	18,700t	40.0%
Equipment	900t	2.0%
Fuel	4,000t	8.4%
Feedwater	530t	1.0%
Defensive weapons	100t	0.2%
Aircraft	100t	0.2%
Total	46,980t	100.0%

Main Weight Groupings in percentages (after Witte)

Ship's hull	25.4	25.4
Armour	38.1	38.1
MI	6.1	6.1
MII	3.1	3.1
Weapons inc. aircraft armament	16.5	16.5
Instruments and supplies	1.2	1.2
Crew, effects and provisions	1.0	1.0
Potable and washing water	0.7	0.7
Boiler feedwater	0.4	0.4
Fuel	7.5	7.5

Stability values: metacentric height (GM)	40,200t = 3.60
	43,700t = 3.55
	45,951t = 3.87
	47,200t = 4.00
	50,956t = 4.23
	53,200t = 4.40
Maximum stability at angle of list	40,200t = 35°
	43,700t = 34°
	47,200t = 33°
	53,200t = 31°
Limit of stability (centre point)	40,200t = 53°
	43,700t = 55°
	47,200t = 59°
	53,200t = 65°

Armour

The armour plate was principally KC (Krupp Cemented, containing 0.34% carbon, 3.78% nickel, 0.31% manganese and 2.06% chrome) steel, classified Ww=Wotan (soft) or Wh=Wotan hard. Wh had an ultimate tensile strength of 85–95 kg/mm^2, 20% expansion and a yield point of 50–55 kg/mm^2. Ww had an ultimate tensile strength of 65–70 kg/mm^2, 25% expansion and a yield point of 38–40 kg/mm^2.

Belt armour		300 mm KC reducing to 270mm (above) and to 170mm (below)
Citadel		145mm KC with 50mm teak base
Outer skin	(forward)	60mm Wh welded
	(rear)	80mm Wh welded
Longitudinal splinter bulkhead in upper ship		25mm Wh welded
Armoured transverse bulkhead beneath armour deck between torpedo bulkheads		200mm Wh
Armoured transverse bulkhead up to platform deck from outer skin to torpedo bulkhead		100mm Wh
Armoured transverse bulkhead beneath platform deck between torpedo bulkheads		80mm Wh
Armoured transverse bulkhead beneath upper platform deck between torpedo bulkhead and outer skin		20mm Wh
Longitudinal torpedo bulkhead		45mm Ww, riveted
Armour deck		80mm Ww, riveted
Armour deck above ammunition rooms		100mm Wh
Armour deck in forecastle		30mm Wh
Armour deck astern		80mm Wh
Armour deck above rudder machinery		100mm Wh
Upper deck		50mm Wh welded
Upper deck near control tower		80 Wh welded
Barbettes for 38cm turrets		340mm KC (middle, forward), 340mm KC (sides), 340mm KC (rear); *Tirpitz* 220mm KC (rear)
38cm turrets		360mm KC (face), 220mm KC (sides), 320mm KC (rear), 180mm KC (roof, forward), 130mm KC (roof, rear)
15cm turrets		100mm KC (face), 40mm KC (sides), 40mm KC (rear), 40mm KC (roof)
10.5cm		20mm shields
Forward control tower		350mm KC (sides/slope), 200mm KC (roof), 220mm KC (communications shaft), 70mm KC (deck)
Aft control tower		150mm KC (sides/slope), 50mm KC (communications shaft)
Upper belt armour		145mm KC
Slope of belt armour, midships and ends		320mm KC on *Bismarck*, 315mm KC on *Tirpitz* (and reducing to 170mm)

Decks:

Upper deck above machinery, centre	50mm Wh (*Bismarck* and *Tirpitz*)
Upper deck above magazines, centre	80mm Wh (*Bismarck* and *Tirpitz*)
Slope above machinery	110mm Wh (*Bismarck* and *Tirpitz*)
Slope above magazines	110mm Wh (*Bismarck* and *Tirpitz*)
Armour deck above machinery, centre	80mm Wh (*Bismarck*); 50mm Wh (*Tirpitz*)
Armour deck above magazines, centre	95mm Wh (*Bismarck*); 100mm Wh (*Tirpitz*)
Slope above machinery	110mm Wh (*Bismarck* and *Tirpitz*)
Slope above magazines	120mm Wh (*Bismarck* and *Tirpitz*)
'A' turret at depth of 3.05m	Thickness of bulkhead 53mm Torpedo bulkhead 45mm
'B' turret at depth of 3.51m	Thickness of bulkhead 53mm Torpedo bulkhead 45mm
Midships to depth of 5.5m	Thickness of bulkhead 53mm Torpedo bulkhead 45mm
'C' turret to depth of 3.35m	Thickness of bulkhead 53mm Torpedo bulkhead 45mm
'D' turret to depth of 3.05m	Thickness of bulkhead 53mm Torpedo bulkhead 45mm
Control tower rangefinder	100mm KC (horizontal) 200mm KC (slope)
Aft control tower rangefinder	50mm KC (horizontal) 150mm KC (slope)
Foretop	20mm (horizontal) 60mm (sides)
Rangefinders	20mm KC (horizontal) 50mm KC (sides)

Underwater protection: The ship's armour was resistant to an explosive charge of 250kg TNT. The depth of armour was 5.5m, the thickness of the longitudinal bulkheads 53mm. The overall bottom protection system had a depth of 1.7m. The citadel was resistant to a hit by a 38cm shell weighing 1,016kg fired from ranges between 10,793m and 21,031m (for the machinery) and from 23,319m (for the magazine).

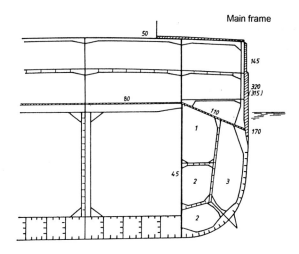

1 = Feedwater cell; 2 = Fuel bunker; 3 = Wall passage

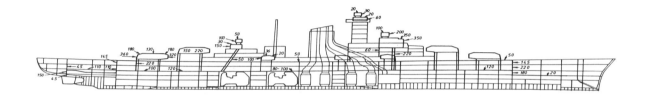

Above: Arrangement and distribution of armour.

Armament

	Bismarck	*Tirpitz*
Main	8 × SK 38cm/L47	8 × SK 38cm/L47
Secondary	12 × SK 15cm/L55	12 × SK 15cm/L55
Flak	16 × 10.5cm/L65	16 × 10.5cm/L65
	16 × 3.7cm/L83	16 × 3.7cm/L83
	12 × 2cm	12 × 2cm (78 × 2cm by July 1944)
Torpedo armament	None	2 banks 53.3cm quadruple mountings from end 1941 to early 1942
Ammunition inventory:		
Main armament	840–960	840–960
Secondary armament	1,800	1,800
Flak	6,720 × 10.5cm	6,720 × 10.5cm
	32,000 × 3.7cm	32,000 × 3.7cm
	24,000 × 2cm	24,000 × 2cm
Torpedoes	Nil	24

Note: As the war progressed, stocks of ammunition aboard *Tirpitz* increased, particularly for the main guns and the flak. By 1944 she carried over 90,000 rounds of 2cm. Abbreviation SK = *Schnellade/Schnellfeuerkanone* (quick-loading/quick-firing gun). L is

Left: *Bismarck* in the final phase of fitting out. This is 'D' turret. Notice the turret armour, the thickness of which can be judged by the protruding end of the rangefinder. In German naval practice, the main turrets are identified alphabetically 'A' ('Anton'), 'B' ('Bruno'), 'C' ('Caesar'), 'D' ('Dora') and so on. The alphabetical/numbering system of the ship's weapons runs from forward to aft whereas the ship's rooms and compartments are numbered from astern forward.

the length of the gun barrel expressed in terms of the calibre. Thus 38cm/L47 = a barrel length of 17.86m. The term *'Flak'*—a contraction of *Fliegerabwehrkanonen*—is used throughout this book to describe anti-aircraft (AA) weapons and installations both aboard ship and ashore.

Armament Details

Calibre	Barrel length (m)	Wt of shell (kg)	Muzzle velocity (m/sec)	Range (m)	Elevation of barrel	Rds/ barrel/ min	Chassis
38cm/L47 C34	17.86	800	820	36,510	−8° to +35°	2	C34 roller track platform
15cm/L55 C28	8.25	45.3	875	23,000	−10° to +40°	8	C34 roller track platform
10.5cm/L65 C33	6.825	15.1	900	17,700	+85°	18	*Bismarck*: four forward, triaxially stabilised twin mounting C31, stern C37; *Tirpitz*: triaxially stabilised twin mounting C37
3.7cm/L83 C30	3.071	0.745	1,000	6,750	+80°	80	Twin mounting C30
2cm/L65	0.9	0.132	900	4,800	+90°	200 single, 800 quad	Basic mounting C38: on *Tirpitz* later quadruple C38 mounting; *Bismarck* had 2cm C30 single mountings and a C38 2 × 2cm quadruple

Note on barrel data: Foreign sources supply different particulars: 38cm/L52 and /L48.6 The former is the total length of the gun in calibres including chassis and breech block, and the latter the actual barrel length. The same applies to the 15cm/L55 and /L52.4: the former agrees with the German specification, the latter gives a barrel length of 7.816m.
10.5cm/L65 and /L60.5: the former agrees with German specification, the latter is 6.348m.
3.7cm/L83 and L80: the former corresponds to German length of 3.071m, the latter to 2.96m.
2cm/L65 is 0.9m according to German sources and 1.3m according to British sources.
'C' indicates the year in which a gun or chassis type was first built (e.g. C34 = 1934).

Right: Four minesweeping paravanes were carried, two each on either side of the aft superstructure deck, and were used in conjunction with the bow protection gear. Notice the 'swan's neck' ventilation pipes on the upper edge of the deck.

Fire Direction and Radar Equipment

Base rangefinder	Serving	Location	Radar equipment	Location	Remarks
10.5m	Main armament	'A' turret 'B' turret 'C' turret 'D' turret			Instrument in 'A' turret on *Bismarck* removed in winter 1940/41; never installed on *Tirpitz*
	Main/secondary armament	Foretop revolving dome			
	Main/secondary armament	Aft control centre			
7m	Main/secondary armament	Control tower/ bridge, revolving dome			
6.5m	Main armament	Turret SII Turret PII			
4m Type SL8	10.5cm flak	One either side of control tower; two midships aft			State-of-the-art rangefinders ('Waggletops') with small-radius gyro-horizontalisation, a further development of the gyroscopically stabilised SL6 type
	3.7cm flak	On gun			Manual backsight device
	2cm flak	On gun			Manual backsight fitment
			FuMO 23	Revolving dome, aft control centre	*Bismarck* and *Tirpitz*
			FuMO 212/213 (Würzburg)	Aft control centre	*Tirpitz*: in spring/summer 1944 platform raised by about 2m
			FuMO 23	Revolving dome, foretop with 10.5m rangefinder,	*Bismarck* and *Tirpitz*
			FuMO 23	Bridge dome with 7m rangefinder	*Bismarck* and *Tirpitz*
			FuMO 27	Above 10.5m base rangefinder	Additional installation on *Tirpitz* with supplementary observer platform
			TIMOR	On fighting top roof portside	Additional aboard *Tirpitz* until spring/summer 1944, when replaced by:
			FuMB 4 SAMOS		
			FuMO 26	Foretop	Also replaced two FuMO 23 and FuMO 27
			FuMO 30 Hohentwiel	On fore topmast	FuMO 26 and FuMO 30 on *Tirpitz* from spring/ summer 1944

Technical Plant

Boiler installation: 12 Wagner high pressure steam-heated boilers (with two Saacke burners at one end of each), natural water circulation through six boiler rooms.

Per boiler:
  Evaporation heating surface: 380m²
  Superheater heating surface: 120m²
  Air pre-heat surface: 685m²
  Feedwater pre-heating temperature: 160°C
  Operating pressure: 55 atmospheres forced
  Intervention pressure, safety valves: 58 atmospheres forced (maximum 63)
  Authorised pressure: 68 atmospheres forced

Main safety valves:
  Boiler drum, intervention pressure, steam collector: 68–69.5 atmospheres forced
  Superheat intervention pressure: 66.5–68 atmospheres forced (hot water/steam production process)

Steaming weight: 50 tonnes/hour dry
Boiler efficiency: 80%
Steam temperatures:
  Saturated   287°C
  Superheated   450°C
Heat generated: 31.8kcal/kg
Evaporation figure: 11.8 at 9,300kcal/kg
Steam production: 132kg per m² of surface

Gas resistance: 220mm
Capacity: 144m³
Weight of boiler with water: 52.8 tonnes
Weight of (warm) water content: 4.85 tonnes
Pre-heating temperature (air): 335°C
Furnace load (10^6): 2kcal/m³/hr

Machinery

3 sets geared turbines (Curtis type) with single reduction: in three turbine rooms (*Bismarck* Blohm & Voss, Hamburg; *Tirpitz* Brown, Boveri & Cie) .

Turbine sets in four housings, turbines/propellers rpm:
  High-pressure (HP) turbine: 2,880/270
  Intermediate-pressure (IP) turbine: 2,880/270
  Low-pressure (LP) turbine: 2,430/190
  High-pressure astern turbine: 2,025/180
  Low-pressure astern turbine: 1,715/190
  Cruising turbine: 4,220/270

The HP astern turbine was contained with the IP ahead drum, the LP ahead and astern turbines were grouped together.*

Performance weight of entire drive: 20.3kg/hp

Main drive: Three shafts with three-bladed propellers 4.7m in diameter

Steering assembly: Two balanced-type rudders with 8° divergence towards centreline

---

*There are a number of differently constructed types of turbine for differing applications, *viz*. the Parsons multi-stage reaction turbine; the Laval impulse turbine with one pressure and one velocity stage; the Curtis velocity-compounded impulse turbine with one pressure stage and multi-velocity stages; and the Zoelly impulse turbine with multi-pressure stages, basically similar in contruction to the Curtis. Shipyards or other manufacturers supplying turbines did so mainly under licence. In *Bismarck* the individual turbine sets were grouped round the gearing. The HP reaction turbine was a Curtis wheel with 40 stages, the IP a double-flow 14-stage reaction turbine and the LP a 9-stage reaction turbine supporting the condenser slung below it, as was customary. The HP astern turbine was a single Curtis wheel, the LP astern turbine was of the divided double-flow type. No cruising turbine was fitted. In *Tirpitz* the individual turbines were similar to those of the *Bismarck* except that the ship was fitted with cruising turbines; the cruising and HP drums were both set at the after end of the main wheel; the IP and LP were simple reaction turbines; and the HP astern turbine was contained in the IP ahead drum at its forward end and the double-flow LP astern turbine was located between the LP turbine block.

Electrical Plant

Two electric plants each of four 500kW generators; two electric plants each with five 690kW turbo-generators, one at 460kW connected to a 400kVA AC generator and one with a 550kVA AC diesel generator.

The Type MWM RS 38 diesel motor (numbered 170093 in *Bismarck* and 170094 in *Tirpitz*) in the plant at (4) in the diagram below was a 6-cylinder four-stroke motor of 300mm cylinder diameter and 380mm piston stroke, running at 600rpm for 460ehp. A 20% overload to 550ehp was possible for half an hour. The generators (Type P23 FA925 10 Spec. BZ in *Bismarck* and Type P23 FA925/10+RP 91 sp. in *Tirpitz*) were manufactured by Garbe-Lohmeyer. (A further development of motors of this type was envisaged for installation in Type XI U-boats.)

Results of dockyard tests for *Bismarck* at a displacement of 43,000 tonnes

Output (shp)	No of boilers in use	Shaft rpm	Speed (kt)	Fuel consumption (gm/hp/hr)
3 × 46,000	12	265	29	325
3 × 38,350	12	250		320
3 × 23,300	9	214		335
3 × 13,000	6	176		370
3 × 8,300	3	151		415
3 × 5,000	3	128		500
3 × 12,000 (astern)	12			

Below: Arrangement of ship's machinery

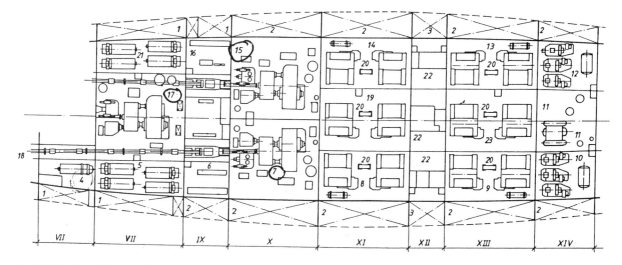

1. Fuel bunkers (diesel oil)
2. Main fuel bunkers (heating oil)
3. Main fuel overflow bunkers
4. Diesel motor room
5. Electric plant No 1
6. Electric switchroom No 1
7. Starboard turbine room
8. Starboard No 1 boiler room
9. Starboard No 2 boiler room
10. Electric plant No 3
11. Auxiliary machinery room
12. Electric plant No 4
13. Port No 2 boiler room
14. Port No 1 boiler room
15. Port turbine room
16. Electric switchroom No 2
17. Centre turbine room
18. Starboard shaft tunnel
19. Centre No 1 boiler room
20. Control platform boiler room
21. Electric plant No 2
22. Boiler auxiliary machinery room
23. Centre No 2 boiler room

Machinery data for *Tirpitz*

Output per shaft	Shaft rpm	Steam consumption (t/hr)
22,500	98	11.5
5,400	130	21.5
11,000	166	39.0
17,500	194	59.0
25,750	220	86.5
34,150	241	114.0
42,750	258	143.3
46,000	265	165.0
16,000 (astern)	190	105.0

Fuel and coolant	Bismarck 1941	Tirpitz 1941
Main fuel, inc. supplementary	8,294t	8,297t
Diesel fuel oil	193t	–
Aviation spirit	34t	–
Reserve feedwater	375t	–
Fresh water	306t	–
Reserve fresh water	389t	–
Lubricating oil	160t	–
	9,751t	

Speeds obtained	Bismarck	Tirpitz
150,170shp	30.1kt	–
163,000shp	–	30.8kt
138,000shp	–	29.0kt

Range	Bismarck	Tirpitz
(Calculations based on trials)	4,500 nm at 28kt	4,728 nm at 28kt
	6,640nm at 24kt	6,963nm at 24kt
	8,525nm at 19kt	8,870nm at 19kt

Below: Looking astern from the forecastle. Notice the broadness of the beam. The photograph was taken in March 1941.

29

Scale Plans

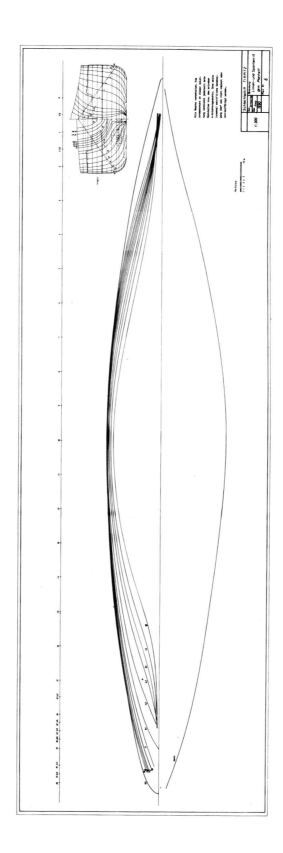

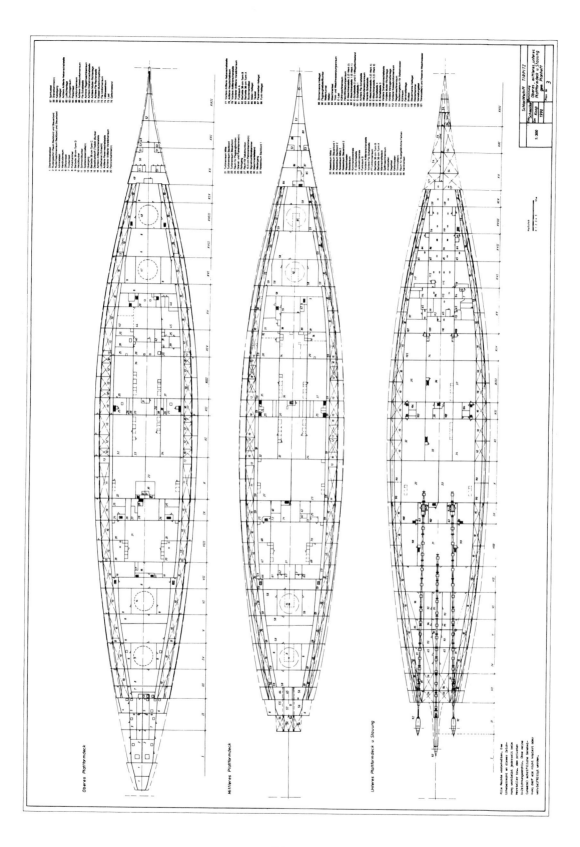

Oberes Plattformdeck

Mittleres Plattformdeck

Unteres Plattformdeck u. Stauung

31

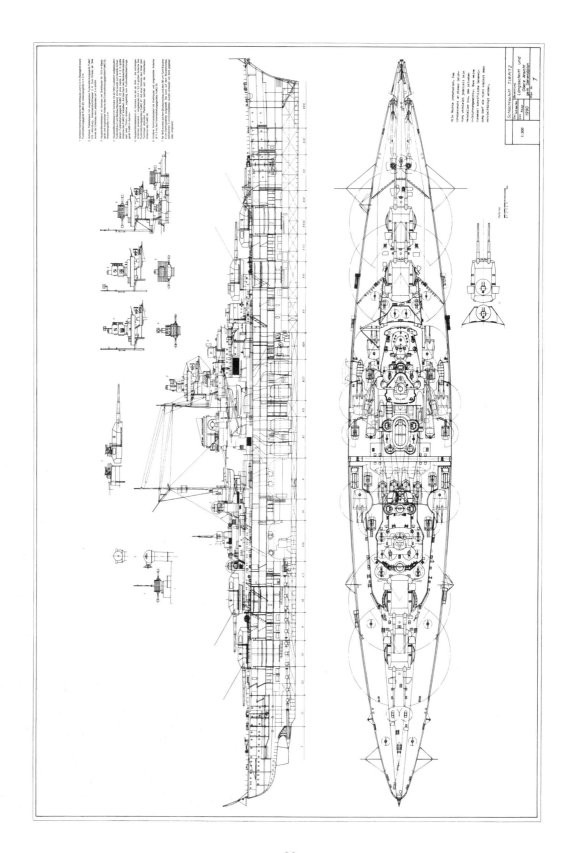

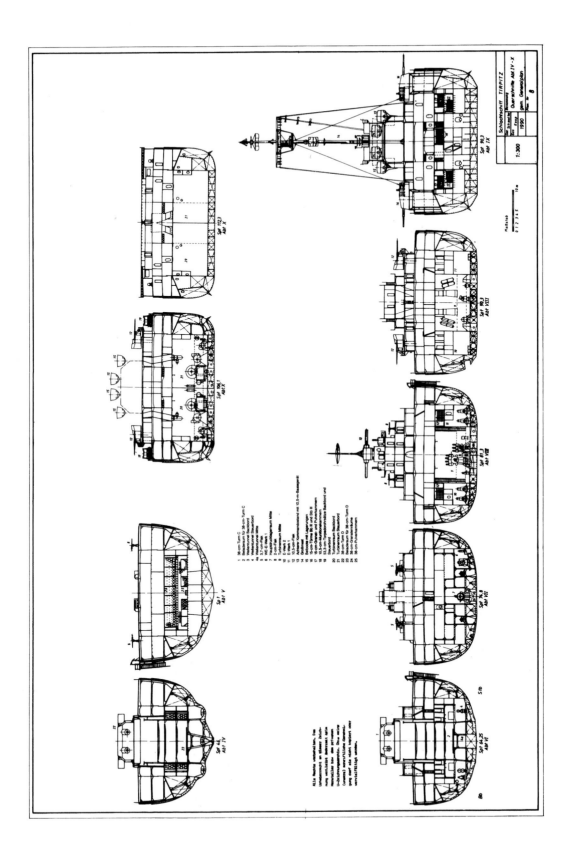

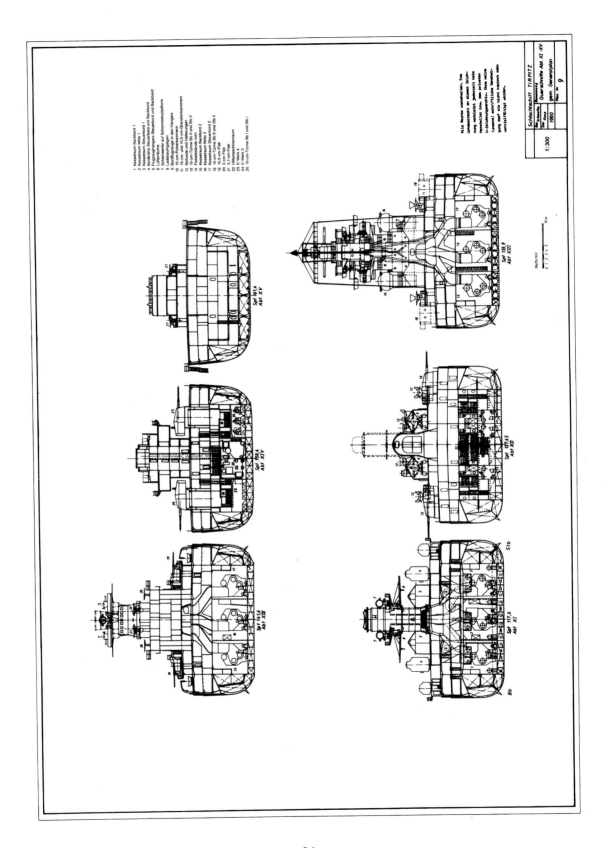

The Battleship *Bismarck*

The building contract for the *Bismarck* was dated 16 November 1935; the keel was laid on 1 July 1936; the hull was launched on 14 February 1939; and the ship was commissioned eighteen months later on 24 August 1940.

After completion of her first trials and a period in the yards for the remaining work to be completed, *Bismarck* was at readiness for operations in the spring of 1941. On 18 May 1941 she sailed from Gdynia to break out into the Atlantic in company with the heavy cruiser *Prinz Eugen*. The operation, code-named *'Rhein-übung'* (Rhine Exercise), was to be the ship's only operation, a combination of triumph and tragedy. The triumph lay in the destruction on 24 May 1941 of HMS *Hood*, the pride of the Royal Navy and up to that time considered to be the largest and most powerful capital ship in the world, with the fifth German salvo of an action lasting only a few minutes. The tragedy came a few days later when, hunted by every available unit of the Royal Navy, she fell victim to a fortuitous torpedo hit on her rudder and, unmanoeuvrable, was eventually battered and overwhelmed by the enemy's battleships.

Below: In the summer of 1940, the ship is almost complete and has been given a final coat of paint. The horizontal line visible along the ship's side is the upper edge of the armour belt, projecting beyond the normal beam of the ship.

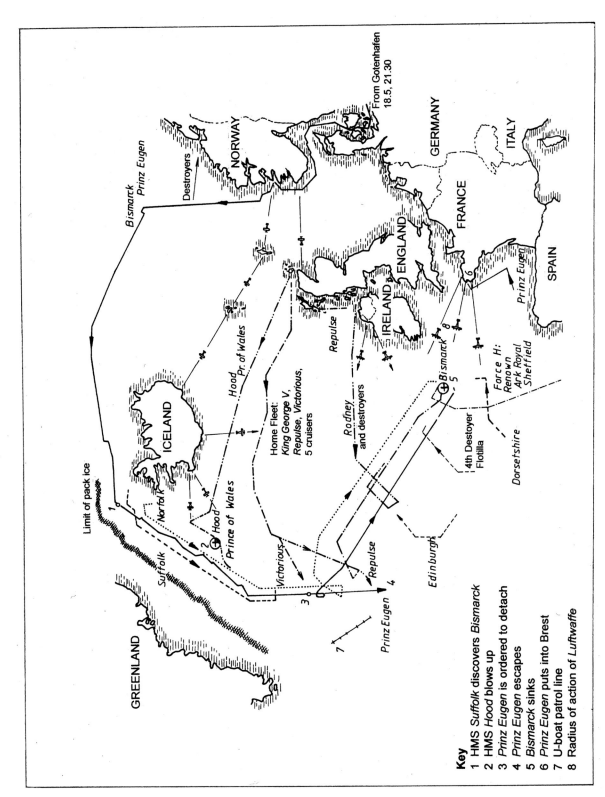

Key

1 HMS *Suffolk* discovers *Bismarck*
2 HMS *Hood* blows up
3 *Prinz Eugen* is ordered to detach
4 *Prinz Eugen* escapes
5 *Bismarck* sinks
6 *Prinz Eugen* puts into Brest
7 U-boat patrol line
8 Radius of action of *Luftwaffe*

'Rheinübung', 21–27 May 1941

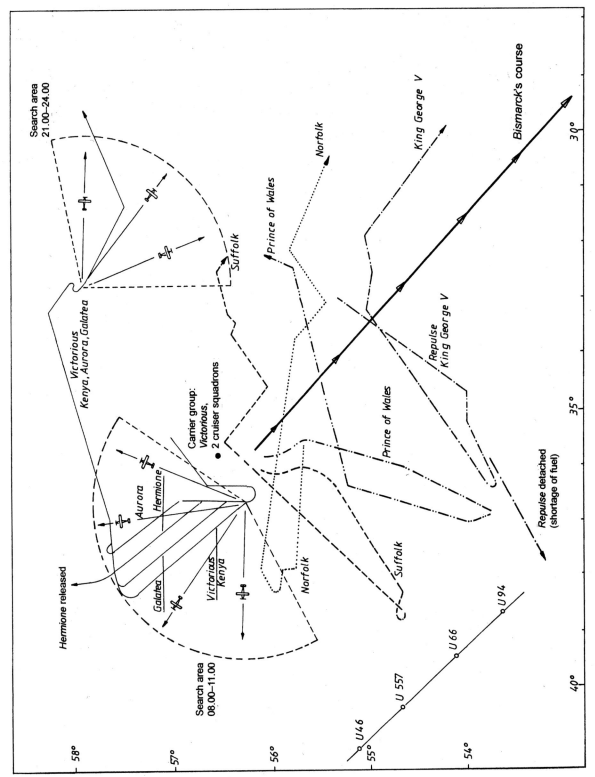

The search for *Bismarck*, 25 May 1941

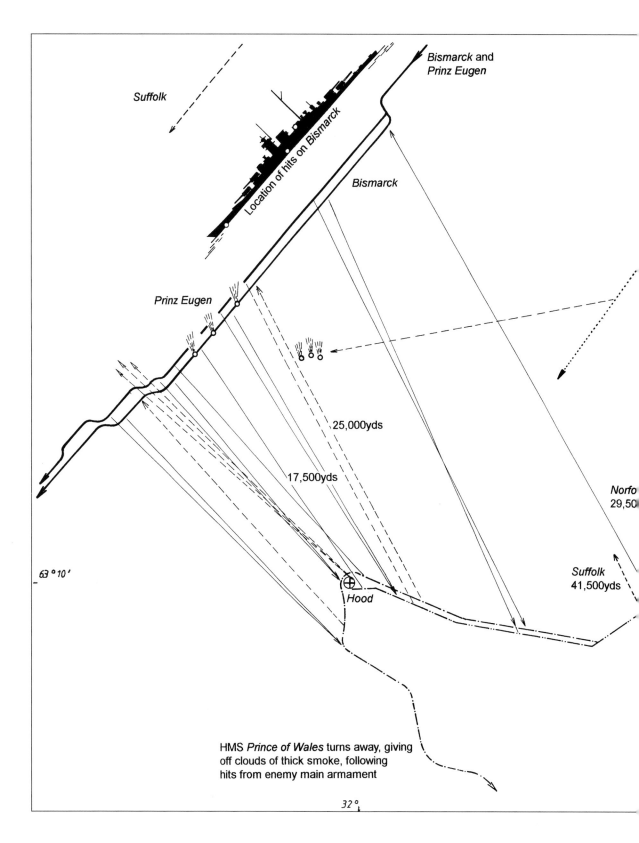

Suffolk

Bismarck and
Prinz Eugen

Location of hits on Bismarck

Bismarck

Prinz Eugen

25,000yds

17,500yds

Norfo
29,50

63°10'

Hood

Suffolk
41,500yds

HMS *Prince of Wales* turns away, giving
off clouds of thick smoke, following
hits from enemy main armament

32°

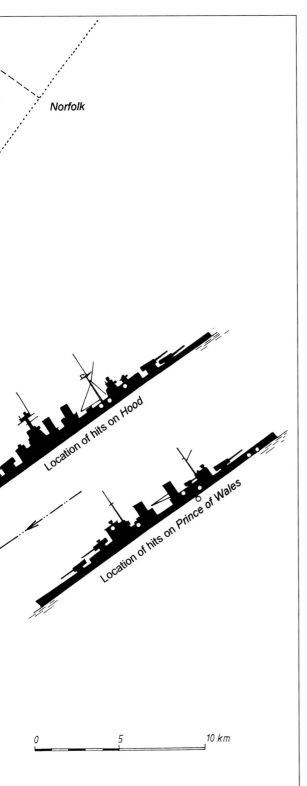

Norfolk

Location of hits on Hood

Location of hits on Prince of Wales

0   5   10 km

Only 115 members of the ship's company were saved: 1,977 men, including the Fleet Commander, *Admiral* Günther Lütjens, and the ship's commander, *Kapitän zur See* Ernst Lindemann, lost their lives. The Commander-in-Chief of the Home Fleet, Admiral Sir John Tovey, who led the hunt for *Bismarck*, praised the German ship, its officers and crew highly.

In 1989 *Bismarck*'s wreck was discovered by investigative divers at a depth of 4,750m. She lies on an even keel, minus her main turrets which became unshipped as she sank. The hull does not appear badly damaged. The location is being kept secret to prevent the wreck from being plundered. The German government has declared the wreck a war grave.

SENIOR OFFICERS (August 1940–May 1941)

Commander	*KptzS* Ernst Lindemann
Executive Officer (IO)	*Fkpt* Hans Oels
Navigation Officer (NO)	*KKpt* Wolf Neuendorf
Senior Artillery Officer	
(IAO)	*KKpt* Adalbert Schneider
Chief Engineer (LI)	*KKpt (Ing) Dip-Ing.* Walter Lehmann

Left: The Battle of the Denmark Strait, 24 May 1941.

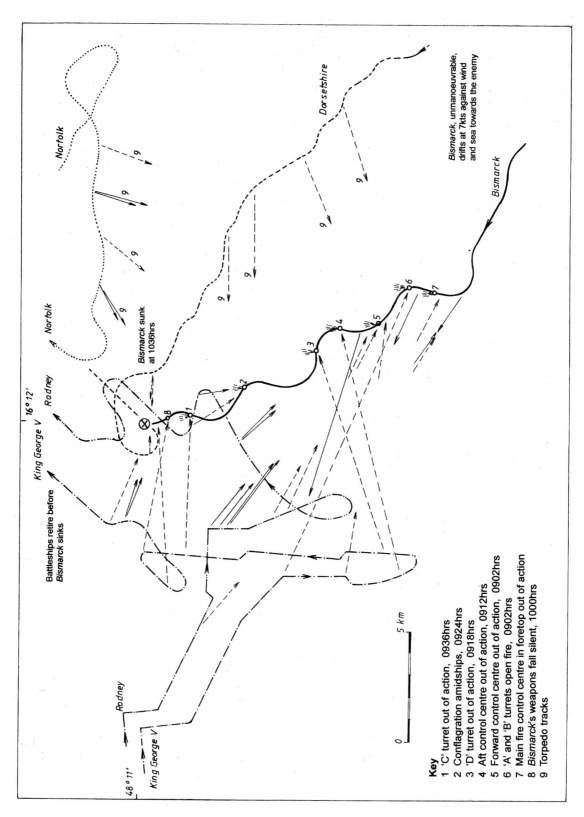

Key
1 'C' turret out of action, 0936hrs
2 Conflagration amidships, 0924hrs
3 'D' turret out of action, 0918hrs
4 Aft control centre out of action, 0912hrs
5 Forward control centre out of action, 0902hrs
6 'A' and 'B' turrets open fire, 0902hrs
7 Main fire control centre in foretop out of action
8 *Bismarck's* weapons fall silent, 1000hrs
9 Torpedo tracks

0   5 km

Bismarck's final battle.

Origin of the Name: Otto Fürst von Bismarck

Otto von Bismarck was born on 1 April 1819 on his father's estate at Schönhausen near Stendal (Brandenburg). After obtaining his law degree in 1835, he served at the Berlin municipal court and in 1837 as a judicial assessor at Aachen. He left government service in 1839 and assumed administration of the family estate at Kniephof, and later at Schönhausen. Bismarck was what one would term a Prussian *Junker* in the positive sense of the expression, loyal to the king but otherwise free and independent.

In 1847 he became a Conservative member of the United Prussian Parliament, and that year married Johanna von Puttkammer, to whom he remained devoted throughout his life. From 1849 to 1850 he was a member of the comparatively insignificant Erfurt Union Parliament.

In 1851 the king appointed Bismarck Prussian representative and envoy to the Federal Diet of Frankfurt and in 1859 he was sent as ambassador to St Petersburg. He fulfilled the same function in Paris, but in 1862, the year of the latter appointment, he was recalled by Wilhelm I on the advice of the Minster for War, von Roon, and installed as minister president in charge of foreign affairs. He immediately clashed with the majority Liberal Party and, with a vehemence to which the Lower House was not accustomed, forced through the king's military appropriations bill and thus, through this constitutional conflict, forestalled Wilhelm's humiliation. This engendered a close relationship of mutual trust between Bismarck and the king which was never weakened, even by Bismarck's occasional violent outbursts and the differences of opinion that arose between them concerning affairs of state.

In 1863 Bismarck prevented Prussia's participation at the Congress of Princes in Frankfurt (here by dissuading the king from attending) because he feared that Prussia would be outvoted and committed to a scheme designed to perpetuate Austrian ascendancy in Germany. He supported the Czar in suppressing a Polish rising and thus laid the foundations for Russo-German friendship which endured for as long as Bismarck set the guidelines for foreign policy.

In 1864, together with Austria and a few of the German federal states, he took Prussia to war against Denmark over the proposal of the latter to incorporate Schleswig into the Danish dominion in breach of the London Treaty of 1852.

In 1866 he prosecuted a war against Austria even though the remainder of Germany, with the exception of Mecklenburg and a handful of the smaller North German states, had sided with Vienna. At its successful conclusion, in the face of the violent opposition of the king and the General Staff, he devised the lenient Peace of Prague to spare Austria humiliation. Until the death of the king Bismarck succeeded in upholding the primacy of politics over the military. In 1867 Bismarck was appointed Chancellor of the North German Federation.

Following the declaration of war on Prussia by France in 1870, Bismarck led the 'German wars'

against France in the 1870–71 period: under the imprint of victory, he devised the First German Reich with the German princes ('Unity from above') against the immediate opposition of Wilhelm I, who in the foundation of a Reich correctly foresaw the eclipse of Prussia. Bismarck became *Reichskanzler*, the only minister of the Reich (who stood alone at the head of the Imperial Administration including all the government departments) and simultaneously Prussia's minister president. The concept of the enlarged North German Federation was the basis for the new German Reich.

Until the death of Wilhelm I in 1888, Bismarck, who considered the Reich as sated and likely to be preoccupied for several decades with internal reconstruction, conducted a foreign policy that was distinctly peaceable. By virtue of its geographical position in central Europe the First Reich was very exposed, and Bismarck sought to safeguard its borders by a complicated system of federations.

On the death of Wilhelm's successor, the ailing Frederick III, who reigned for only 99 days, the crown passed to the former's grandson, Wilhelm II. The differences between the new Emperor and Bismarck in home, social and foreign policy, quite aside from a conflict caused by the evident generation gap, were very substantial. Strained relations developed between the old Chancellor, unable to come to terms with an age of new technology, and his young, self-confident and ambitious emperor. In 1890, the latter intrigued for, and received, Bismarck's resignation. Bismarck died in Friedrichsruh on 30 July 1898.

Particularly after 1945, Bismarck was sharply attacked as a direct 'spiritual' ancestor of Adolf Hitler and was alleged to bear some of Germany's guilt for both World Wars. Nowadays one can see that there is no true comparison between the moderate Bismarck, mindful of preserving peace, and the unbridled hegemony of Hitler. Bismarck was a Prussian and always considered himself to be such, as also did his king and emperor, Wilhelm I. His idea of a *'Kleindeutschland'*, a Reich with limited borders under the stewardship of Prussia, and excluding Austria, obviously bears no valid comparison with Hitler's concept of a *'Grossdeutschland'* that was intended eventually to subjugate all Europe.

The three legs of Bismarck's 'internal policy' were (a) the constitutional conflict (*Verfassungskonflikt*) in the 1860s against the Liberals; (b) the struggle for civilisation (*Kulturkampf*) against the Centre (including the Catholic Church); and (c) the social insurance legislation in the 1880's against the Social Democrats. Only in the first of these was he successful. If it was the purpose of his unique, pioneering social legislation to undermine the growing social democratic movement, in this he failed. On the other hand, his foreign policy has been described in the following terms: 'A blessing he was for Europe! His foreign policy after 1871 was the politics of peace—a policy which, after Bismarck, Germany neither knew nor understood for decades to come, and has only recently rediscovered. It is only now becoming clear how difficult an art is the policy of peace in a world of sovereign states and rival great powers, and one can begin to admire the wealth of imagination and virtuosity with which Bismarck pursued it and the mastery with which he brought it about.' (Sebastian Haffner, in Haffner/Venohr, *Preussische Profil*, Frankfurt am Main/Berlin, 1986)

Right: This photograph, taken on 10 September 1938, shows the embryonic *Bismarck* on the Blohm & Voss slipway. The hull is complete to the level of the upper deck. The barbettes for the 38cm forward turrets ('A' and 'B') are clearly visible, and in the background are 'C' turret barbette and the barbettes for the 15cm secondary armament.

Above: Immediately following the christening of the ship, a board bearing the ship's name, *Bismarck*, is swung over the side to hang at the top edge of the starboard forecastle. The hull braking shields differ in design from those of *Tirpitz*.

Left: *Bismarck* during fitting-out. Here the rotating floor for one of the four 38cm turret barbettes is being lowered into position.

Above: *Bismarck* alongside the Blohm & Voss fitting-out pier in January 1940. Towering behind the ship is one of the large hammer cranes used to load aboard the heavier equipment. The work is well advanced: the main turrets, funnel and conning tower have been installed and temporary structures are in position for the next stage of the building programme.

Right: A view astern from the tower mast, with the funnel in the foreground. Most of the upright cylinders protruding from the base of the cowling are emergency steam release pipes from the ship's boilers, functioning as safety valves.

Above: The final stage of fitting out. The deck and superstructure are still strewn with the electrical cabling carrying power for the dockyard workers' tools and welding gear.

Left: After commissioning: a view into one of the numerous decks, here a leading seamen's mess. Between the two framed pictures on the sloping panel, a notice gives the precise location of the deck by frame number etc. The panelling conceals cables and piping and the information enables the site to be readily identified to technical personnel in the event of breakdown or damage.

Above: *Bismarck* leaves Hamburg for the Baltic via the Kiel Canal, 15 September 1940. The fire control systems for the main and secondary armament have yet to be installed on the foretop and on the command centres fore and aft.

Above: *Bismarck* at Kiel in September 1940. The plume of black smoke probably signifies that the boilers have been fired preparatory to leaving the mooring buoy: notice the ship's boat near the buoy and the absence of the national flag from the jackstaff. The battle ensign is hoisted at the stern. The ship's boats off the quarter appear to be waiting to be brought inboard by crane once their crews have re-joined the ship by the accommodation ladder.

Above: *Bismarck* at high speed in the autumn of 1940.

Above: *Bismarck* sails from Hamburg in the autumn of 1940 still minus her rangefinders and mattress-like radar aerials.

Above: The after command centre with its 10.5m rangefinder and turntable-mounted FuMO 23. The photograph was taken in the spring of 1941.

Right: A view of the bridge structure, starboard side. The 10.5m stereoscopic rangefinder and FuMO radar 'mattress' have been installed at the foretop. The 3.7cm flak twin forward of the bridge superstructure is manned but the SI 15cm turret is at rest.

Above: *Bismarck* alongside at Gdynia in April 1941, wearing the camouflage paintwork customary for the Baltic at that time.

Above: In the roads at Gdynia, 5 May 1941. The ship's company is paraded by divisions facing in close order to starboard for the departure of Adolf Hitler after his visit to the ship. The fenders at the waterline are for the fleet tender *Hela* to come alongside.

Above: A small sailing vessel is overhauled during training in the Baltic between March and May 1941. The barrels pointing skywards are 10.5cm flak twins.

Above: *Bismarck* at Gdynia in the spring of 1941. The two funnels of the old pre-dreadnought *Schleswig-Holstein*, then serving as a cadet training ship, can be seen behind *Bismarck*'s bow.

Above: *Bismarck*, still wearing her Baltic camouflage, sails for Norway in the wake of a mine destructor ship.

Left: A view off *Bismarck*'s bows during her Baltic trials in April 1941.

Above: *Bismarck* off Skagen on 20 May 1941 en route for Norway, as seen from the bridge of a minesweeper. In the background is one of the destroyer escorts, and partially obscured by the searchlight is a minesweeper of the 5th Minesweeping Flotilla, which formed part of the convoy.

Above: *Bismarck* in Grimstadfjord, the last stop before the voyage of no return. By the time she sailed that evening, all her camouflage had been painted over except for the imitation bow wave.

Above: *Bismarck* on 21 May
1941: a stern view taken from
the destroyer *Z10* (*Hans
Lody*).

Left: The break-out through
the Denmark Strait, with *Prinz
Eugen* astern. (From a watercolour by the noted marine art-
ist Zeeden).

Right: The Battle of the Denmark Strait, taken from aboard the heavy cruiser *Prinz Eugen*. Exploding 14in shells throw up great fountains of water in the cruiser's wake.

Right: The Battle of the Denmark Strait, taken from aboard the heavy cruiser *Prinz Eugen*. From her station astern of the cruiser, *Bismarck* fires off a full salvo from her main armament.

Left: HMS *Hood* explodes. In 1941 *Hood* had a standard displacement of 42,462 tons and a load displacement of 48,360 tons. Overall she measured 861ft long, she was 104ft in the beam and her operational draught was 32ft. Her machinery developed 144,000shp, providing a top speed of 31kts. Her armament consisted of eight 15in 42-cal Mk I guns in Mk II twin turrets, fourteen 4in Mk XVI in Mk XIX twin turrets, 24 × 2pdr AA guns (pom-poms) in three eight-barrelled mountings, 16 quadruple mounted 0.5in AA guns and 5 unrifled projectile (AA rocket) batteries with 100 misssiles in crates of 20. (From a watercolour by Zeeden)

Above: *Bismarck* fights off an attack by torpedo aircraft. (From a watercolour by Zeeden)

Above: The end: *Bismarck* is hit by a torpedo from the British heavy cruiser *Dorsetshire*. Shortly afterwards, the battleship went to the bottom of the Atlantic.

Above: The burning *Bismarck*, obscured from the enemy's view.

Above: The launching of *Tirpitz* on 1 April 1939. The photograph gives an impression of the ship's huge size.

The Battleship *Tirpitz*

The Launch

The launch of every ship involves special considerations. In the case of *Tirpitz*, the enormity of the problem of launching was exacerbated by the great size of the hull and the restricted confines of the *Kriegsmarine* dockyard basin at Wilhelmshaven where she would enter the water.

It was therefore essential that the theoretical calculations and tests were in this case particularly thorough. An important point for consideration in ship launchings is the declivity of the groundways, for the longer the ship's hull the greater the pressure on the surface of the slip. The inclination usually ranges from 1 in 12 for smaller ships to 1 in 22 for larger. The declivity of the slipway for the *Tirpitz* was set at 1 in 18, which, having regard to the groundways, was calculated to be the optimum angle of descent for arresting the hull's progress by means of the braking measures once afloat.

There are four consecutive phases to each stern-first slipway launch:

1. Under the force of gravity the ship slides down the greased ways and the lowest point at the stern touches the water surface;

2. The stern begins to immerse until buoyancy reaches the point where the hull is practically afloat;

3. The hull floats freely, having slid off the end of the ways; and

4. Under the momentum of the ride down the slip, the hull makes way through the water.

Stage 1 did not apply to the launch of *Tirpitz*: at the Wilhelmshaven yard the end of the slipway was below the water level, kept dry by gates which were opened on the launch day to flood the lower slip so that the lowest point at the stern was already in contact with the water. During construction calculations had been made to predict the behaviour of the hull during launching and to arrange for vessel and slip-

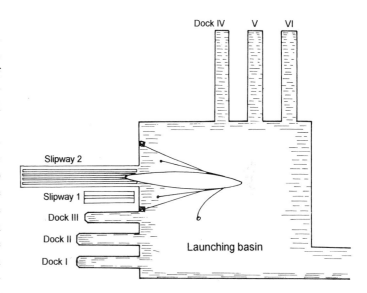

Above: Arrangement of waterbrakes (hull just afloat) on basis of scale model.

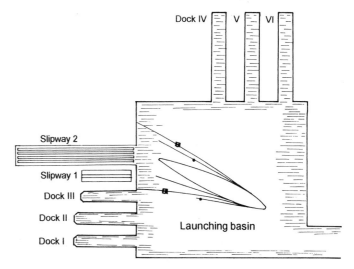

Above: Arrangement of waterbrakes (effect of swivel anchor) on basis of scale model .

way to be in a proper and safe condition. Problems of a similar nature had had to be overcome during the building of *Scharnhorst* on the same slip, and the naval architects were able to draw on the experience.

The launch basin was 376m across, and the nature of the measures necessary to get the hull under control can be imagined if one visualises the forces generated by a colossus the size of *Tirpitz* travelling down the slipway. The kinetic energy is more than 30,000 megatonnes, which far exceeds that of a speeding express train.

The matters to be determined included:
1. The effects of various sizes and settings for the hull waterbrakes;
2. The effectiveness of other braking devices including the retarding power of lines and chains;
3. A calculation of the ship's probable velocity during the launch and the directional sheer of the hull once waterborne;
4. Determining (a) when buoyancy would reach a value sufficient to pivot the ship about the forward end of the launching cradle and (b) when the ship would be freely afloat; and
5. A calculation of the volume of water over the lower slipway.

All theoretical tests and calculations were carried out using two hull models and a model of the launching basin with slipway to a scale of 1:30. As a result of the comprehensive experimentation, it was eventually decided that the hull should be equipped with brake shields, an anchor at bow and stern, braking floats and a swivel anchor.

The launch of 1 April 1939 proceeded without complications. The responsible Admiralty official appointed to the Wilhelmshaven naval dockyard staff was ministerial adviser Hermann Burckhardt, who had also supervised the ship's construction.

Career
1936
The building contract was placed on 14 June with the Kriegsmarine Werft, Wilhelmshaven, as New Construction 'G', Ersatz *Schleswig-Holstein*, Construction No 128, located on Slipway 2, from where, on the previous 3 October, the battleship *Scharnhorst* had been launched. The size of the new ship was such that the slipway had to be lengthened, a reinforcing foundation being laid at its for-

ward end for the purpose. Two dates have been given for the keel-laying, 24 October and 2 November. Both are documented in the German photographic and military archives. Probably the earlier date was the day on which the building work actually began and the later the official keel-laying attested to in photographs.

1939
The launch took place on 1 April in the presence of Hitler, who appeared for the official ceremonies accompanied by a large entourage. Numerous guests, highly placed Party functionaries, representatives from politics, business and industry were also present, together with a crowd of about 80,000 people who thronged the slipway. In addition many military personalities attended, especially from the former German Imperial Navy and the former Austro-Hungarian Navy (Retired Lists): *Adm* Souchon, *Adm* W. von Lans, *VAdm* Looff, *VAdm* Wedding, *VAdm* Boedicker, *VAdm Frhr* von Rössing, *VAdm Staatsrat* A. von Trotha, *VAdm* Löhlein, *VAdm* Rogge, *VAdm* Reymann, *VAdm* von Reuter, *VAdm Frhr* von Gagern, *VAdm* Rösing, *KAdm* Kühlenthal, *KAdm* Pieper, *KAdm* Brüninghaus, *KAdm* O. Lans, *KAdm* Kranzbühler, *KAdm* Saxser, *KAdm* von Fischer-Loszainen, *Staatssekretär KKpt Frhr* von Rheinbaben, *KAdm* Mörseberger, *KAdm* Retzmann, *KAdm* Hering, *KAdm* Hornhardt, *KAdm* von Purschka, *KAdm* Türk, *KAdm* Khuepach, *KptzS* von Stosch, *KptzS* Erler, *Linienschiffskapitän* Dittrich, *FKpt Frhr* von Senarclens-Grancy, *FKpt* Scheibe, *FKpt* Mann, *KKpt* Erich E, Schulze and *Kptlt* von Tirpitz. From the *Reichsmarine* (Reserve List) were *VAdm* Prentzel, *Adm* Heusinger von Waldegg, *VAdm* von Trotha and *VAdm* Bartenbach, and from the *Reichmarine* (Retired List) *VAdm Dr phil h.c.* Groos, *VAdm* Franz, *KAdm* Bindseil, *KAdm* Coupette, *KAdm* Goehle, *KAdm* Seebohm, *KAdm* Claassen, *KAdm* Klüpfel and *AdmRat* Pelte. From the *Kriegsmarine* were *Adm* Boehm, Fleet Commander; *Adm* Witzell, Chief of the Marine Ordnance Office; *VAdm* Marschall, Commander *Deutschland* class *Panzerschiffe*; *VAdm* Densch, Commander Reconnaissance Forces; *VAdm (Ing)* Fechter, Head of Marine Engine Inspctorate; *Adm-oberstabsarzt Prof Dr med* Moosauer, Head of the Naval Medical Office and of *Kriegsmarine* hospitals; *KAdm* Lütjens, Commander Torpedo Boats; *KAdm* von Schrader, 2nd Admiral North Sea Station; *Adm* Albrecht, Commander Naval Group (East); *KAdm* Fuchs; and virtually all Flotilla commanders and commanders of naval land stations.

The pre-launch speech was given by *VAdm* von Trotha and the christening performed by *Frau* von Hassell, daughter of *Grossadmiral* Tirpitz, after whom the ship was named, and wife of Ambassador (Reserve List) von Hassell, who was also present. (The last-named was later to be condemned to death for complicity in the bomb plot of 20 July 1944.)

1941

The ship was commissioned on 25 February. After completing her preliminary trials, *Tirpitz* entered the Baltic, docking at Kiel, and later Gdynia, for completion. Meanwhile the crew underwent a full training programme in order to have the ship battleworthy as soon as possible. Initial problems in the ship's weapons were quickly overcome and her gunnery trials were successfully completed in June.

On 5th May Hitler visited the naval yard at Gdynia—the Commander-in-Chief of the *Kriegsmarine*, *Grossadmiral* Raeder, was conspicuous by his absence—and inspected both *Tirpitz*, alongside the jetty, and *Bismarck*, anchored in the roadstead. Less than a fortnight later, the latter vessel embarked on the maiden voyage from which she would not return.

The Russian Campaign began on 22 June. To prevent the anticipated break-out of Soviet naval forces into the Baltic, the so-called Baltic Fleet, consisting of *Tirpitz*, the heavy cruiser *Admiral Scheer* and the light cruisers *Emden*, *Leipzig*, *Köln* and *Nürnberg*, together with numerous destroyers, torpedo boats and minesweepers, was assembled in September. *Tirpitz* was attached for a short period only, patrolling the area of the Aaland Islands from 26 to 2 September. Subsequently battle training was resumed.

1942

In early 1942, following discussions held at Führer HQ, all serviceable German units of heavy cruiser size and larger were ordered to Norway to pre-empt an Allied invasion there. There was an important merchant convoy route across the Arctic Ocean from Iceland and Scotland to Murmansk and Archangel in the USSR (PQ convoys) and back (QP convoys). (Between 1941 and 1945, 19 PQ convoys (PQ.1–18) made the eastward haul, losing 53 of 276 ships in the process. Sixteen out of 223 ships in QP returning convoys were also lost.)

Tirpitz left Kiel on 12 January 1942, arrived in the Jade estuary after a transit of the Kiel Canal, anchored in the roadstead at Wilhelmshaven, where she was fully refuelled and reprovisioned, and sailed for Norway on the 14th. Escorted by the destroyers *Richard Beitzen*, *Paul Jacobi*, *Bruno Heinemann* and *Z29*, she arrived at Trondheim in a severe snowstorm on 16 January and anchored close inshore along the banks of Aasfjord, a branch of Faettenfjord 30km inland. The width of Aasfjord was about 300m.

Tirpitz was appointed flagship of the battle group formed in the area under the Commander of Battleships, *Vizeadmiral* Ciliax, later under the Commander of Cruis-

ers, *Vizeadmiral* Kummetz. From March to September the Fleet Commander, *Admiral* Schniewind, Commanding Officer of Operation *'Sportpalast'*, a proposed sortie against convoys PQ.12 and QP.8, had his flag aboard the battleship. A squadron consisting of *Tirpitz* in company with the destroyers *Z25*, *Friedrich Ihn*, *Paul Jacobi* and *Hermann Schoemann* left coastal waters on 6 March, two torpedo boats originally included having been ordered back because of the weather. The German group was soon battling into fierce blizzards, nil visibility and appalling seas, and failed to contact the enemy convoy. A Soviet freighter sailing independently which ran across the path of the destroyers was sunk.

The British submarines *Trident* and *Seawolf* reported the German squadron but failed to obtain a favourable attacking position. A squadron of the Home Fleet consisting of the battleships *King George V* and *Duke of York*, the aircraft carrier *Victorious*, the heavy cruiser *Berwick* and destroyers, operating in the area as a distant escort for the convoy, failed to contact the German battle group. *Victorious* flew off aircraft, but these did not press home an attack until the German ships were already heading back for Westfjord/Lofoten. *Tirpitz* avoided all torpedoes fired at her and anchored in Westfjord undiscovered on 9 March. On 12 March she put back to Trondheim and on the 13th made fast to cables at her previous mooring.

In the Norwegian theatre, the acute shortage of fuel imposed periods of idleness for destroyers and larger ships, and activities were restricted to exercises at anchor. The British used this opportunity to mount repeated air attacks, particularly against *Tirpitz*. This task was taken up initially by RAF Bomber Command.

On 27/28 April *Tirpitz* was attacked by 26 Halifax bombers of No 4 Group and 10 Lancasters of No 5 Group, and on 28/29 April by 23 Halifaxes and 11 Lancasters. At this time *Tirpitz* and the heavy cruisers *Admiral Scheer* and *Prinz Eugen* all lay within complexes of anti-torpedo nets. The RAF had previously attempted to knock *Tirpitz* out on 30/31 January with seven Short Stirlings of No 15 Squadron and nine Halifaxes of No 76 Squadron, a second raid being carried out by 36 Halifaxes on 30/31 March. All these attacks were driven off by the heavy flak defence which had been alerted in good time, although the weather was also a contributory factor.

When in mid-June the fuel situation improved, preparations were made for Operation *'Rösselsprung'* which had as its object an attack on convoy traffic. Two groups were assembled—Battle Group I under the Fleet Commander, *Admiral* Schniewind, aboard *Tirpitz*, and Battle Group II under *Vizeadmiral* Kummetz on board the heavy cruiser *Lützow*. The target was convoy PQ.17 with a reported 34 ships escorted by six destroyers, two AA cruis-

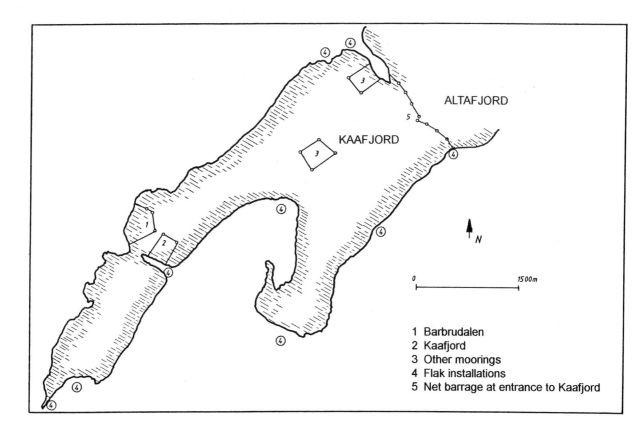

1 Barbrudalen
2 Kaafjord
3 Other moorings
4 Flak installations
5 Net barrage at entrance to Kaafjord

ers, two submarines, four corvettes and 13 other vessels. Two battleships, an aircraft carrier, one heavy and one light cruiser and 14 destroyers of the Home Fleet, to which a further four heavy cruisers and three destroyers were added later, were standing off as distant escort.

PQ.17 was reported by *Luftwaffe* reconnaissance on 1 July, but a QP convoy returning from Murmansk was missed. The next day *Tirpitz*, in company with the heavy cruiser *Admiral Hipper*, the destroyers *Friedrich Ihn*, *Hans Lody*, *Karl Galster* and *Theodor Riedel* and the torpedo boats *T7* and *T15*, later joined by the destroyer *Richard Beitzen*, set off for Altafjord. En route *Hans Lody*, *Karl Galster* and *Theodor Riedel* all grounded and were obliged to drop out. Battle Group II was hit by similar problems. Having assembed in Ofotfjord on 3 July, the heavy cruiser *Lützow* stranded en route to Altafjord and was forced to retire to Bogenfjord. *Vizeadmiral* Kummetz's force had now been reduced to the heavy cruiser *Admiral Scheer*, five destroyers, *Z24*, *Z27*, *Z28*, *Z29* and *Z30*, and the fleet oiler *Dithmarschen*.

The enemy was aware that the German squadron had put to sea, and as a result of a later much disputed assessment of the situation PQ.17 scattered and the escort was withdrawn, the merchantmen being left to attempt to reach their destination independently. This development persuaded the German naval planners to abandon their own operation and recall the various units to Altafjord/Bogenfjord while the ships of the former PQ.17 were savaged by U-boats and the *Luftwaffe* and virtually wiped out.

Tirpitz left Bogenfjord on 23 October to refit at Trondheim, where the necessary technical personnel were available. The work was subsequently carried out in stages. On 30/31 October the first attempt by the British to put the *Tirpitz* out of action by using midget submarines met with no success.

1943

As a consequence of the fiasco of New Year's Eve 1942, when two heavy cruisers, *Lützow* and *Admiral Hipper*, attacking a convoy, were engaged by a British covering force of similar strength and forced to retire in a damaged condition having achieved no success, Hitler ordered all heavy units to be decommissioned and withdrawn to Germany. *Tirpitz* alone was excluded, since she was required to help repulse the anticipated Allied invasion of Norway.

The Commander-in-Chief of the *Kriegsmarine*, *Admiral* Dönitz, promoted to *Grossadmiral* as successor to *Grossadmiral* Raeder following the resignation of the latter in protest at the decommissioning order, succeeding in obtaining a partial remission of the instruction.

From 24 January *Tirpitz* was again fully battleworthy and spent the intervening period to 5 March carrying through trials and exercises in nearby waters. On 11 March, in company with the heavy cruiser *Prinz Eugen* and escorted by the destroyer *Karl Galster* and the torpedo boats *Jaguar* and *Greif*, she moved up the coast from Trondheim to Bogenfjord near Narvik and met up with the battleship *Scharnhorst* and the heavy cruiser *Lützow*.

On 23 March *Tirpitz*, *Scharnhorst*, *Lützow* and six destroyers transferred to Altafjord, where the squadron carried out exercises until July.

In September the Germans mounted Operation *'Sizilien'*, which had as its objective the Allied bases and installations on the island of Spitzbergen. On the 6th *Tirpitz*, *Scharnhorst* and the destroyers *Z27*, *Z29*, *Z30*, *Z31*, *Z33*, *Erich Steinbrinck*, *Karl Galster*, *Hans Lody* and *Theodor Riedel* weighed anchor in Altafjord/Kaafjord and headed for Spitzbergen. This was one of the few occasions when the enemy remained in the dark about a German naval operation. At moorings the units were always on display to any casual passer-by. There were no restrictions on the movements of the Norwegian population—and their numerous agents—and it was a simple matter to obtain information for clandestine transmission to the enemy.

Installations on Spitzbergen were destroyed or set ablaze in the concentric fire of the German weapons and storm troops disembarked from the destroyers saw to the remainder with explosives. By 9 September *Tirpitz* was safely back at Altafjord.

The standing threat which the *Tirpitz* represented was a constant worry for the British, especially for the Royal Navy, which carried the main burden in the Battle of the Atlantic. The ship's mere presence obliged the Royal Navy to keep at readiness substantial forces which were needed much more urgently elsewhere. Accordingly they renewed their efforts to eliminate *Tirpitz*. As the RAF had failed in its attempts so far, the Royal Navy took up the initiative.

Operation 'Source' represented a further attack on the battleship using midget submarines. A total of six X-craft were towed most of the way by standard submarines. Not all the force arrived, and only *X6* and *X7* successfully placed their explosive charges below *Tirpitz*'s hull amidships. *X6* was discovered prematurely and sunk; *X7* was sunk while attempting to escape. The rescued British submariners kept silent, and *Tirpitz*'s commander remained unaware of the exact nature of his ship's predicament, but he ordered all watertight doors closed as a precaution.

At 0812hrs on 23 September the first charge exploded on the port side about 6m from the midships engine room, followed shortly afterwards by a second explosion, 61m abaft the port bow, while desperate attempts were being made to kedge the battleship off the anchorage by means of her stern anchor windlass.

The damage sustained was very extensive: a failure of nearly all electric lighting, partial flooding of electric switchboard room 2, flooding of the double bottom and and fuel bunkers on the port side, a 1-degree list to port (quickly corrected by counterflooding) and one generator only available to supply electrical power, the remainder having damaged steam pipes or severed cables. In the engine plant there was structural damage to the housing and components of the port turbine and condenser (LP astern turbine); the tail shafts were out of alignment, the thrust bearing was damaged, and the ship's propellers were immobilised; and the port rudder assembly was flooded through insecure stuffing boxes. The main gun turrets had been jolted from their roller tracks, the gunhouse flooring of 'A' and 'B' turrets, closest to the explosions, would require weeks of repair and the after Port III 15cm turret was jammed fast. The only rangefinder still intact was that at the foretop: 'B' turret rangefinder had been demolished, and those on the control tower and 'C' turret, together with the secondary rangefinders, required replacing. Both fire control centres aft were damaged, and only one of the forward centres remained operative. The aircraft catapult could not be used and two floatplanes had been seriously damaged. Casualties were, however, slight, with one dead and 40 wounded.

This operation, which had begun on the night of 22 September 1943, succeeded in putting *Tirpitz* out of commission for the first time, presenting the *Kriegsmarine* with a very difficult situation. As it was impossible in the circumstances to have the disabled battleship towed to Germany for repairs, it was decided that the work would have to be carried out in Norway alongside the repair ship *Neumark*. A dockyard workforce of about 1,000, together with the necessary specialists such as naval divers, was brought out from Germany aboard an accommodation ship, the former liner *New York*. All replacement parts also came from Germany. The ship's bottom was partially sealed with cement while repairs to the shaft, stern stuffing boxes and other underwater work was carried out using cofferdams. New rangefinders were cannibalised from the incomplete heavy cruiser *Seydlitz* or supplied from the shore inventory. The repairs lasted into the spring of 1944.

1944

Once the Royal Navy had succeeded in hunting down and destroying the battleship *Scharnhorst* while the latter was engaged on an anti-convoy sweep off the North Cape on Boxing Day 1943, it focused all its attention on eliminating *Tirpitz*. The task was taken up by the Navy because sufficient carriers and suitable aircraft had recently become available.

On 10/11 February Soviet bombers mounted an unsuccessful attack on *Tirpitz*, which in the months since the X-craft attack had reached a stage in her repairs enabling her to begin trials on 15 March. The degaussing gear was checked over, and following various trials in Barbrudalen and Altafjord, during which *Tirpitz* logged a top speed of 27kts, the ship was signed off as combat-ready. Meanwhile the Royal Navy had been building up its force of aircraft carriers in the area. *Victorious*, *Furious*, *Emperor*, *Pursuer*, *Searcher* and *Fencer* carried, in all, 42 Fairey Barracudas, 28 Vought Corsairs, 20 Grumman Hellcats, 40 Grumman FM-1 Wildcats, 14 Supermarine Seafires, 8 Grumman F4F-4 Wildcats and 12 Swordfish torpedo-bombers.

Between 7 and 15 March several planned attacks were postponed on account of inclement weather, but on 3 April the two waves of aircraft flown off in Operation 'Tungsten' met with success. Warning of the raiders' approach had been given only at the last moment, and the aircraft arrived over the target at 0528hrs with the element of surprise. They encountered only sporadic flak and little smoke cover over the target, and were able to press home the attack. They had a new tactic: before the bombs were dropped, the escorting fighters strafed the ship and and exacted a heavy toll amongst the unprotected flak gunners.

The second attack followed at 0636hrs and was carried out in the same manner as the first. Ten Hellcats and 20 Wildcats took part, the Barracudas putting in a repeat appearance. The losses in personnel aboard the *Tirpitz* were 132 dead and 316 wounded, two of whom were dockyard workers. *Tirpitz* expended 506 rounds of 10.5cm, 400 rounds of 3.7cm and 8,260 rounds of 2cm ammunition. The bombs dropped by the attackers were as follows:

Below: Location of hits and near-misses scored on *Tirpitz* during the attack of 3 April 1944.

	1st attack	2nd attack
500lb SAP bombs	24	39
500lb GP bombs	12	9
500lb A/S bombs (for mining effect)	4	2
1,600lb AP bombs	7	2

The following damage to the *Tirpitz* resulted from 16 hits or near-misses: a near miss to the starboard boiler room aft; a hit on 'B' turret; a hit on the quarterdeck in area of 'D' turret; a hit by a bomb which penetrated down to armour deck level above the port turbine room; a hit on the port hangar which detonated in the officers' messrooms and another which damaged the funnel and caused fires; a hit on officers' accommodation aft in the vicinity of SI 15cm turret; a hit below the armour belt which made a gash 4.5m long and an entrance hole 1m by 0.5m in the outer skin; damage to sthe tarboard keel plates and frame system, with a total of 15m of welded seams burst; a hit through the port deck, two hits through the upper deck, and one near PI 15cm turret causing fires in the region of the upper deck and putting the turret out of action; and a near miss on the starboard shaft mountings.

Despite this comprehensive damage the main armament remained fully serviceable. The dockyard personnel required about a month for repairs below the waterline, and the *Tirpitz* was ready for trials by 1 July. The first of these had actually been scheduled for 22 June but fell victim to a renewed fuel shortage so severe that it also put a stop to the customary snap interchanges of moorings between the German heavy units.

The Royal Navy was not satisfied with the scale of damage inflicted during the double attack of 3 April, but a fresh onslaught planned for 24 April under the code-name 'Planet' and involving 40 Barracudas and 40 escort fighters had to be shelved because of the conditions, the weather in high northern latitudes being subject to drastic fluctuations. A similar fate befell Operation 'Brawn', involving 27 Barracudas and 36 fighters, and also 'Tiger Claw' on 28 May, and it was not until 17 June that the next mission against the *Tirpitz* could be flown.

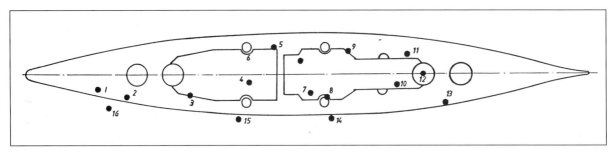

The 44 Barracudas, 18 Hellcats and 30 fighters involved in Operation 'Mascot' took off from the carriers *Formidable*, *Indefatigable* and *Furious* but they were detected very early on and by 0219hrs *Tirpitz* had been forewarned. By the time the raiders arrived, every gun was manned and the smokescreen so thick that the aircraft failed to penetrate the defences. *Tirpitz* expended 39 × 38cm shells, 359 rounds of 15cm, 1,973 rounds of 10.5cm, 3,967 rounds of 3.7cm and 28,500 rounds of 2cm ammunition.

Tirpitz carried out exercises at sea for the last time, with the destroyers *Z29*, *Z31*, *Z33*, *Z34* and *Z39*, on 31 July and 1 August. On 22 August the carriers *Formidable*, *Indefatigable*, *Furious*, *Nabob* and *Trumpeter* flew off 32 Barracudas escorted by 43 fighters in the double operation 'Goodwood I' and 'II'. This proved unsuccessful, and the attack was driven off. *Tirpitz* expended the following ammunition: 75 rounds of 38cm (the shells were time-fused to explode 20,100m from the ship), 487 rounds of 15cm, 2,000 rounds of 10.5cm, 4,000 rounds of 3.7cm and about 20,000 rounds of 2cm. The ship suffered one fatality on board and 10 wounded.

A subsequent attack under the code-name 'Goodwood III' carried out by 33 Barracudas, 10 Hellcats, 5 Corsairs and 29 fighters from the carriers *Indefatigable*, *Furious* and *Formidable* on 24 August resulted in two hits, one destroying the 2cm quadruple flak mounting on the roof of 'B' turret and the other entering at bridge level on the port side and penetrating down five decks to the platform deck, where it came to rest in switch centre 4 and failed to explode. The bombs had been released at a height of 1,500 metres. *Tirpitz* fired off 72 rounds of 38cm, 510 rounds of 15cm and about 40 per cent of the light flak. There were eight dead and 13 wounded. The incoming attack had been detected at 1535hrs when the aircraft were 63 miles distant, the alarm was raised aboard the battleship at 1541hrs and *Tirpitz* was screened with smoke by 1600hrs.

On 29 August 26 Barracudas, 2 Corsairs, 7 Hellcats and 25 fighters repeated the attack in 'Goodwood IV' but *Tirpitz* was warned well in advance and the aircraft, finding the ship completely blanketed by smoke, were forced to bomb blind. There were a number of near misses and *Tirpitz* had six wounded, and damage was limited to one 10.5cm ammunition hoist destroyed. *Tirpitz* used 54 rounds of main ammunition and 161 rounds of 15cm, plus 20 per cent of her flak. Up to this time, in 95 passes by bombers and 73 by their fighter escorts, 52 tons of bombs had been aimed at *Tirpitz*, but the ship remained battleworthy.

Her approaching demise was finally signalled on 15 September, when RAF Bomber Command resumed its involvement in the effort to destroy *Tirpitz* using a special type of bomb for the first time. On 10 September 36 Lancaster bombers took off from Lossiemouth in Scotland for Archangel in the Soviet Union, from where the attack, code-named Operation 'Paravane', was to be mounted. These were aircraft of Nos 9 and 617 Squadrons, No 5 Group Bomber Command; No 617, the 'Dambusters', had established its reputation in May 1943 in the attacks on the Möhne and Eder dams. Of the 36 aircraft, only 23 actually made it to Murmansk airfield, the others having landed elsewhere after straying as a result of faulty navigation. Nevertheless 27 machines started out on 15 September, 21 of them each carrying a 12,000lb bomb known as a 'Tallboy' and the rest loaded with twelve 400lb JW-II mines.

Tirpitz received early warning and was fully screened by the time the bombers arrived, forcing them to drop into the smoke: she received one direct hit which penetrated the deck forward of the chain stopper on the forecastle, exited through the bow plating and came to rest on the bed of the fjord close to the keel about 10.5m abaft the forefoot, where it exploded and caused serious damage, not least a hole in the stem 9.7 by 14.6m in size. A section of the bow between the forepeak and the armoured bulkhead 36m abaft it had been devastated, while some of the decks had been forced upwards, the armoured deck by a metre. The forecastle was 2.4m down by the head as a result of flooding. The ship was eventually trimmed by redistributing some of the fuel oil and flooding side compartments aft. It was calculated that 1,500 tons of seawater was washing round the ship. The explosion had seriously damaged the hull and all turbines would be out of action for a week.

Many optical fire control instruments were out of commission and the radar aerials on the tower had been damaged. As the aircraft alarm aboard had been raised in good time, casualties were limited to five wounded, and all available guns, including 98 sited on the surrounding mountain-tops, had maintained an effective defensive barrage.

Tirpitz was no longer seaworthy. Following a full inspection of the damage, it was estimated that repairs, including a new bow, would take nine months. Initially only the ship's weapons were fully serviceable, followed later by the machinery. As a result of discussions in Germany on 23 September it was decided not to proceed with the repairs but to retain the battleship as a floating gun emplacement in a defensive location to be specially prepared for that purpose.

A position in Lyngenfjord on the south shore of the island of Haakøy near Tromsø was chosen. An initial survey of the anchorage showed a depth of 12m beneath the keel and a rocky bottom with a 1m thick layer of sand, but subsequently it was discovered that the true depth was 17m beneath the keel, that the bottom was not rocky, and that the supposed layer of sand was actually a much thicker layer of mud. Accordingly it was decided to entrench the bottom directly under and around the ship inside the anti-submarine net complex. A total of 28,000 cubic metres of sand was required for this purpose. It is now apparent that the second marine survey was not carried out with any thoroughness. Two matters had been overlooked: the anchorage was uneven, and, fatally, there was a huge hole towards its centre which the Norwegians traditionally used as a fishing ground. The Germans foresaw that in the event of a capsize, at worst *Tirpitz* would roll through no more than 90 degrees and come to rest on the shore alongside. Instead, it was her misfortune that when the capsize began, the mast/funnel complex rolled into the hole, thus causing an almost complete inversion.

After emergency repairs had been carried out to the stem, the ship was able to steam at 10kts, and on 15 October she made the overnight voyage south from Kaafjord to her new anchorage. On 18 October she was photographed there by Fireflies of 1771 NAS flown from HMS *Implacable* and a Mosquito aircraft of No 540 Squadron, and as a result 32 Lancasters of Bomber Command executed Operation 'Obviate' on 29 October. *Tirpitz* was given early warning but was able to set only a partial smokescreen because of the weather conditions. Nevertheless the British aircraft were again bombing blind, and all their 12,000lb bombs were wide, with only one near miss which exploded about 15m off the port side in the region of the steering gear, buckling the outer plating and destroying the outer stuffing boxes of the port shafting with resultant flooding over a 35m stretch of the stern on that side.

From this time *Tirpitz* was, indeed, nothing more than a floating gun emplacement. She received additional flak protection ashore and from the flak ships *Nymphe* and *Thetis* (the former Norwegian armoured ships *Tordenskjold* and *Harald Haarfagre* respectively), which were anchored nearby. All surplus materials and weapons (torpedo warheads, aviation spirit and aircraft parts and ammunition) and crewmen (predominantly technical personnel with the exception of boiler and turbo-generator specialists) were now disembarked, and no more repairs were planned. The attack of 29 October had blown the port shafting off alignment, and this could not be repaired without its removal: the port rudder was damaged, which meant that the ship was unmanoeuvrable. From 2 November the dredgers began the shoring work beneath the ship. This work was only half complete by 11 November, for the 'earthquake bombs' which had missed the ship on 29 October had altered the contours of the bed of the fjord.

On 12 November 2 Lancasters of Nos 9 and 617 Squadrons, carrying 29 12,000lb bombs, took off from Lossiemouth for Operation 'Catechism'. *Tirpitz* was given the first warning at 0800hrs and was at full battle-readiness by 0900hrs. For reasons still not clear today, the *Luftwaffe* airfield at Bardufoss appointed to the defence of *Tirpitz* failed to put up fighter cover and the battleship was left to fight off the enemy aircraft alone. The bombers were still 13.5 miles distant at 0938hrs when they began to encounter the shrapnel barrage from *Tirpitz*'s two main forward turrets, supplemented by fire from the 15cm and 10.5cm barrels at 9.5 miles. The first bombs fell at 0941hrs.

The ship received two direct hits, both on the port side, one near 'B' turret and the other midships, which penetrated the armour deck and exploded in a boiler room, creating a 14m hole from the bilge keel to the upper deck through which the sea rushed into boiler rooms I and Centre and the port turbine room. The ship assumed a list of between 15 and 20 degrees. A near miss detonated off the bow.

Within the next three minutes the ship was hit again, on the port side near PIII 15cm turret, and also suffered the effects of a near miss close to PI 15cm turret which destroyed the watertight integrity of PII boiler room and the magazine and shell handling room of PII 15cm turret. Another hit, in the magazine and handling room of PIII 15cm turret, caused leaks through to the aft gyro compass room

Below: The last station: *Tirpitz*'s final anchorage, based on an RAF aerial reconnaissance photograph of 18 October 1944.

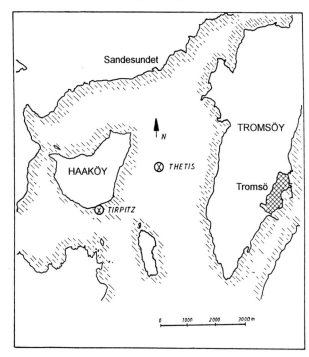

Right: The end of the *Tirpitz*, 12 November 1944. The sketch shows chronologically the impact point of each 'Tallboy' bomb aimed at the ship. Bombs 12, 13, 15 and 16 fell outside the area shown.

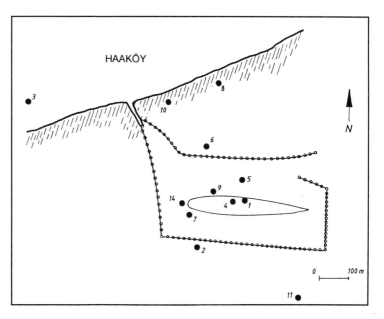

and fan room. By now approximately 67m of the port side was flooded and the ship had a list of 40 degrees, so that the sea was lapping the edge of the upper deck. At 0945hrs the order was given to evacuate the lower decks. Despite the terrible damage and the heavy losses amongst flak personnel, the machine guns continued firing.

By 0950hrs the list had increased to 70 degrees. The hit on PIII 15cm turret had set off a fire which could not be extinguished, and on reaching 'C' turret magazine it resulted in an explosion which blew the gunhouse into the air. At 0952hrs *Tirpitz* capsized and settled on the bottom at an angle of 135 degrees. Altogether 971 crew members lost their lives; 806 were saved, and a further 82 were eventually brought out alive from the upturned hull.*

The wreck of *Tirpitz*—together with that of the heavy cruiser *Blücher* in Oslofjord and about forty other wrecks of various kinds—was purchased after the war by a former Norwegian Resistance fighter, allegedly for 75,000 kroner. As he and his fellow entrepreneurs then ran out of money, their interest in the wrecks was sold to the Hamburg firm Eisen & Metall. Work on scrapping *Tirpitz* resumed in 1951.

The main monument to the battleship is in Wilhelmshaven, where the *Tirpitz* survivors meet annually to lay a wreath at the military cemetery, to attend a memorial service at the garrison church and to remember the ship's dead.

---

*According to *Der Scheinwerfer* , the information broadsheet of the battleship *Tirpitz* shipboard community, No 2, December 1989.

SENIOR OFFICERS
Commanders

Feb 1941–Feb 1943	*KptzS* Karl Topp
Feb 1943–May 1944	*KptzS* Hans Meyer
May 1944–Nov 1944	*KptzS* Wolf Junge
Nov 1944	*KptzS* Robert Weber

Executive Officers (IO)

Feb 1941–Oct 1942	*Fkpt* Paul Friedrich Düwel
Oct 1942–Aug 1943	*KptzS* Heinz Assmann
Aug 1943–May 1944	*KptzS* Wolf Junge
May 1944–Nov 1944	*KptzS* Robert Weber

Navigation Officers (NO)

Feb 1941–May 1941	*KKpt* Werner Hoppe
May 1941–Mar 1942	*KKpt* Gerhard Bidlingmaier
Mar 1942–Feb 1944	*KKpt* Kuno Schmidt
Feb 1944–Apr 1944	*KKpt* Hugo Heydel
Apr 1944–Sep 1944	*FKpt* Hans Henning von Salisch
Sep 1944–Nov 1944	*KKpt* Gerfried Brutzer

Senior Artillery Officers (IAO)

Feb 1941–Sep 1943	*FKpt* Robert Weber
Sep 1943–Nov 1944	*KKpt* Willi Müller

Chief Engineers (LI)

Feb 1941–Oct 1942	*FKpt (Ing)* Oskar Stellmacher
Oct 1942–Sep 1943	*FKpt (Ing)* Paul Steinbüchler
Sep 1943–Nov 1944	*FKpt (Ing)* Alfred Eichler

Camouflage Schemes

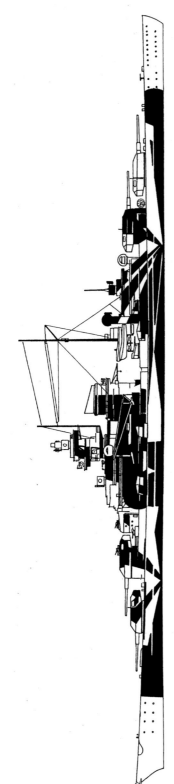

Port profile, July 1942

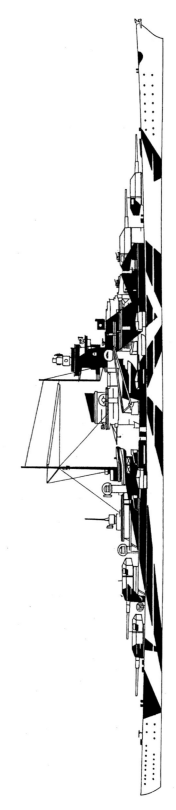

Starboard profile, March 1944

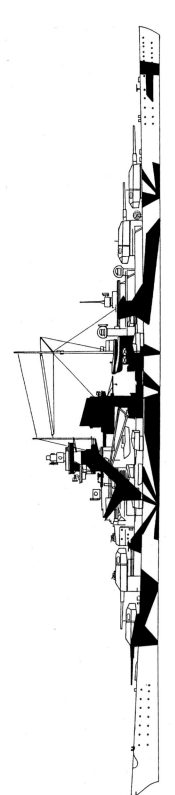

Port profile, March 1944

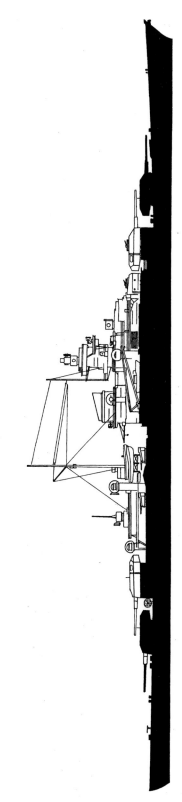

Starboard profile, May–August 1944

Origin of the Name: *Grossadmiral* Alfred von Tirpitz

Born on 19 March 1849 in Küstrin, Brandenburg, Tirpitz passed the examination for acceptance as a naval cadet on 1 April 1865 in Berlin (Crew 65) and entered the Prussian Navy on 24 June 1869. On 22 September 1869 he was promoted to *Leutnant zur See*. Between 1877 and 1889 he was prominently involved in the building up of the Torpedo Arm, and although on the Admiralty staff was also a member of the Torpedo Experimental Commission. During this period he commanded the yacht/torpedo ship *Zieten* and from 1877 to 1885 was Executive Officer and subsequently commander of the flush-decked corvette *Blücher* (which doubled as a torpedo experimental vessel).

On 17 September 1881 Tirpitz was promoted to *Korvettenkapitän* and from January 1885 to March 1886 he was head of the Admiralty's torpedo section. From April 1886 to April 1889 he was First Inspector of torpedo gunnery, and from 1885 to 1887 he was also Commander of the Torpedo-Boat Flotilla. On 24 November 1888 he was promoted to *Kapitän zur See*. He commanded the armoured ships *Preussen* from April 1889 to May 1890 and *Württemberg* from May to September 1890.

From January 1891 to January 1892 he was Chief of Staff at the Naval Station, Baltic, and during this period, as Chief of Staff of the Autumn Fleet Exercise, with the assistance of the commanding admiral, *Freiherr* von der Goltz, he enunciated the principles of Fleet tactics and deployment, later known as Service Booklet IX. On 13 May 1895 he was promoted to *Konteradmiral* and in March 1897 he became Secretary of State at the Office of the *Reichsmarine*, where he remained until March 1916.

On 28 March 1898 Tirpitz was appointed a Prussian Minister of State and on 5 December 1899 he was promoted to *Vizeadmiral*. On 12 June 1903 he was promoted to *Admiral* and on 27 January 1907 was awarded the Order of the Black Eagle (*Schwarzenadlerorden*). Promotion to *Grossadmiral* followed on 27 November 1911, and on 10 August 1915 he was awarded the Pour le Mérite. He resigned on 15 March 1916 in protest at the undertaking by the German Government not to engage in unrestricted submarine warfare. Tirpitz died on 6 March 1930 at Ebenhausen near Munich.

The German Navy at the outbreak of the First World War represented the lifetime's work of Alfred von Tirpitz. It was his conviction, shared by his contemporaries (a fact which should not be overlooked by modern critics), that the new and expanding, technologically and economically flourishing German Reich required a large Fleet. This belief was also held by the *Kaiser*.

The case was made that Germany's acquisition of colonies (which Bismarck had renounced) created the need for overseas naval bases, which would serve the twofold purpose of protecting the colonies and ena-

70

bling the navy to 'show the flag' around the world—principles in line with the imperial aspirations of both the *Kaiser* and Tirpitz. While both of them naturally appreciated that the dream of building a war fleet greater in size than that of Great Britain was not feasible, it became the policy to build a Fleet sufficiently powerful as to represent a substantial risk for Great Britain should the latter embark upon armed conflict with Germany. Tirpitz's 'Risk Theory' led to the German High Seas Fleet later being referred to by historians as the *'Risikoflotte'*. The idea that Britain might view this German Fleet as something of a menace does not appear to have occurred to Berlin.

Contrary to what the Germans had anticipated, however, Britain's entry into the Great War on the side of Germany's enemies demonstrated that the British would indeed take the risk, as they proved again at Jutland on 31 May/1 June 1916. Despite the German tactical successes resulting from outstanding training programmes, this battle was not the German victory it was proclaimed to be, for the British won the operational and strategic aspects of it. The German High Seas Fleet had not succeeded in modifying any of the geographical disadvantages under which it was obliged to operate (the 'Wet Triangle'), and would, from now on, skulk in port, outwardly quiet but inwardly simmering towards the revolt out of which the revolution would come. Tirpitz had not advocated this policy: he had always wanted to 'strike with the Fleet'. But the *Kaiser* would not have it, and before Jutland Tirpitz knew he had to go.

For their part, the British steered clear of the 'Wet Triangle' and blockaded Germany instead. Final victory was theirs. Over a short period of time, Tirpitz had created, within limits, a usable weapon: any blame that the full political preconditions for its deployment had not been met fell less on Tirpitz than on the shoulders of the *Kaiser*, who had, ultimately, the total political responsibility.

In the Second World War, the false assessment of Britain's response and the daydream of a fleet that was far beyond Germany's capabilities to build (the famous Z-Fleet of the *Wehrmacht*), with the ultimate goal of becoming a world naval power, were errors which had tragic parallels in the First World War.

Above: Wilhelmshaven, Slipway 2: *Tirpitz*'s first keel plates have been laid.

Above: Slipway 2: already the staging of the hull has risen up like a wall. To the left, an auxiliary vessel lies across the end of Slipway 1; further to the left can be seen dry docks II and III, in the first of which a destroyer can be made out.

Above: Looking down the stern of Battleship 'G' towards the launching basin. The raised barbette of 'C' turret and the side barbettes for the 15cm turrets are easily recognisable. Beyond the cranes is the old pre-dreadnought *Hannover*.

Above: This photograph from the 1946–47 period shows that the foundations of the strengthened and lengthened Slipway 2 survived the destruction and dismantling of the Naval Yard. The slip itself has already been filled in. The Shipbuilding Hall beyond it remained and is part of the present day naval complex.

Above: Another view of the foundations of the extended No 2 Slipway. Visible to the left of the photograph, immediately in front of the terracing of houses, is the office of the site manager responsible for the strengthening work.

Above: The Rathausplatz, Wilhelmshaven, 31 March 1939: banner- and standard-carrying formations of the NSDAP rehearse for the following day's march past.

Above: The great day arrives: the Rathausplatz, 1 April 1939. The launching ceremony will take place, and Hitler is to deliver a speech here.

Left: Adolf Hitler speaks, standing at a lectern protected for the first time by armoured glass. It has often been said that in this speech he abrogated the Anglo-German Naval Treaty, but this is incorrect as the treaty was not nullified until the 23rd of that month.

Right: A view from outside the yards. The upper stem and forepeak rear massively upwards, seemingly towering above the roof of the Ship-building Hall. The height of the hall and of the terrace of houses (still standing today) on the other side of the street both provide a good indication of the size of the ship.

Right: *Tirpitz*'s 'godmother', *Frau* von Hassell, holds the obligatory bottle of champagne ready for the christening.

Above: The state ceremony runs its course: with a pull on the thin line from below, the ship's heraldic device is unveiled. On the lower platform are numerous invited guests of honour; on the podium stands Hitler with an small entourage.

Left: This stern view gives a good indication of the ship's massive 36m beam.

Right: Dressed overall from stem to stern, with the line of pennants supported by two temporary pole masts forward and aft, *Tirpitz* leaves the stocks.

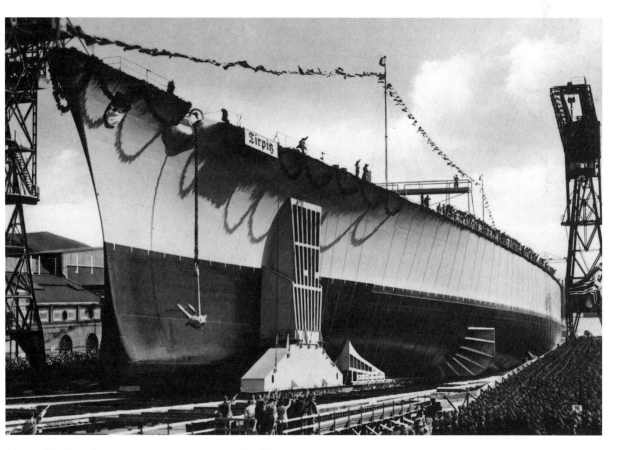

Above: Slowly at first, then gathering speed, the ship slides into her new element. The large waterbrakes on the port side, plus the smaller ones further down, and the huge swivelling anchor merit special notice.

Above: As soon as the ship has become waterborne, her progress is impeded by tugs arranged to bring the vessel gradually to a standstill before she is manouevred to an anchorage. Clearly visible on the slip are the four sliding ways required for her huge beam.

Left: The tugs have brought the enormous hull under control and slowly begin the turning manouevre.

Above: The fitting-out basin. Its size can be estimated by reference to *Tirpitz*'s hull. The pre-dreadnought *Schleswig-Holstein* occupies Dock IV.

Above: *Tirpitz* completing alongside the south quay of the fitting-out basin behind the large *'Langer Heinrich'* floating crane. This photograph shows the harbour canal leading into the dockyard.

Above: From the beginning of the Second World War, the British took pains to obtain information by aerial reconnaissance and then to check the yard's activities by bombing raids. In the lower part of this photograph, taken on 30 August 1940, the square body of water is the fitting-out basin. *Tirpitz* is made fast at the south quay and the heavy cruiser *Admiral Hipper* at the east quay. In the right upper corner is the building site of the new IV harbour entrance with its two chambers and, at an angle to the left, the construction site of the planned northern yard with a good view of the large dry docks VII, VIII and IX.

82

Above: A photograph taken in the winter of 1939–40 looking south across the fitting-out basin. The minelayer *Cobra* is in the foreground, while *Tirpitz* can be seen still completing alongside the south quay.

Right: Fitting out. Here the funnel mantle is being installed: the platforms are to accommodate four searchlights. In the foreground is the barbette for a 38cm turret.

Above: This was the view across the harbour canal on 2 February 1940: behind the pedestrian swing-bridge for the dockyard personnel is the bulk of *Tirpitz*, with bridge foundations fitted and cylindrical tower mast mounted. Alongside her is the *'Langer Heinrich'* floating crane, while building cranes can be seen on the pier.

Above: Fitting-out progresses: a view looking aft from above the starboard side. To the right of the picture can be seen the walls of the starboard hangar, to the left and further astern two 15cm turrets, and on the centreline, astern, the barbettes for the 38cm gun turrets. Around the centre of the ship are many covered openings through which various equipment such as engine parts can be lowered into the interior. Dry docks I–III are visible in the background; to their right are stagings on slipway 1, apparently for the recently begun light cruiser 'N', work on which was abandoned soon after the outbreak of war.

Above: Fitting-out proceeds: the tower mast now has many platforms and the main gun turrets have been fitted.

Left: The 38cm guns are lowered aboard.

Right: One of the massive 38cm guns prior to installation.

Above: A photograph taken in the winter of 1940–41 showing the bridgework/funnel complex almost complete, some of the ship's boat stowed aboard, searchlights installed on the funnel platform and covered with tarpaulins and the two forward flak-control positions fitted. The main gun turrets, secondary turrets and 10.5cm flak mountings are fully equipped and in position.

Above: The ship nears completion and is camouflage-painted to represent a barracks, from which even the window details have not been omitted.

Above: This view shows the ship in the final stages of fitting-out.

Above: Before being commissioned, *Tirpitz* went back into dock for a final coat of paint and the removal of hull accretions and fouling which had accumulated during the long period in the brackish water of the fitting-out basin. The ship's company was now mustered aboard.

Above: *Tirpitz* passes the Kaiser Wilhelm Bridge, Wilhelmshaven's most famous landmark.

Above and below: *Tirpitz* in the 40,000-tonne floating dock at the Wilhelmshaven Navy Yard.

Right: Wilhelmshaven, 25 February 1941: the battleship *Tirpitz* is commissioned. Her commander, *KptzS* Topp, greets a delegation of the yard workers involved in the ship's construction, and offers them his thanks. The weather is cold and windy, with snow showers.

Right: The commander goes aboard and the Executive Officer, *FKpt* Düwel, reports the ship's company on parade.

Right: The guard of honour presents arms while drummer and bugler stand by.

Left: The ship's officer corps.

Left: A view of the forecastle, port side, with the ship's company assembled in divisions. A 2cm flak gun can be made out in front of the breakwater.

Left: A view over the quarter-deck. The ship's company is paraded for the flag-hoisting ceremony. No 1 dry dock is astern of the ship's counter.

Above: The ship's company from the stern rail.

Right: 'Hoist ensign and pennant!': the commissioning.

Left: The commander salutes the battle ensign; the guard of honour presents arms; the strains of the national anthem break out; and the ship is taken into commission.

Above: Just a few days after commissioning, following the completion of her engine and speed trials, *Tirpitz* leaves Wilhelmshaven, never to return. Assisted by several tugs, she is seen here in entrance III, skilfully negotiated by her officers and the tugmasters. The ship is not yet fully fitted out: amongst other items still ashore is the entire fire control system for the main armament. It is just possible for *Tirpitz* to exit through the lock system, but only the North Chamber Lock, 250m long, 40m wide, and 11m deep at normal high water, is large enough.

Above: *Tirpitz* at Kiel for the resumption of fitting-out. The photograph shows her close by the extended bridge of the naval complex.

Above: A view from the port side showing the ship enmeshed in camouflage netting as a counter to enemy reconnaissance. The large rangefinders have now been installed.

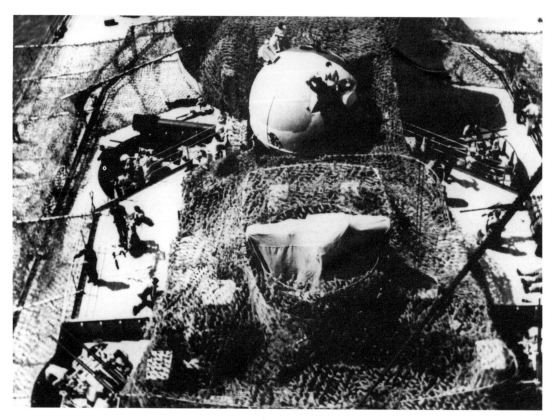

Above: A view down to the aft flak fire control position and the aft command position from aloft. The camouflage nets mask other structures, but the 2cm and 3.7cm flak mountings are nevertheless at readiness.

Above: In addition to the rangefinders the ship receives mattress-like aerials for FuMO 23 radar, which are visible here on the command bridge and facing to port atop the fire control centre. They are mounted on the front faces of the revolving domes of the rangefinders.

Above: Fitting out was completed later at Gdynia. Here *Tirpitz* is alongside a pier in one of the many large basins of the harbour. The early camouflage scheme has given way to a uniform grey.

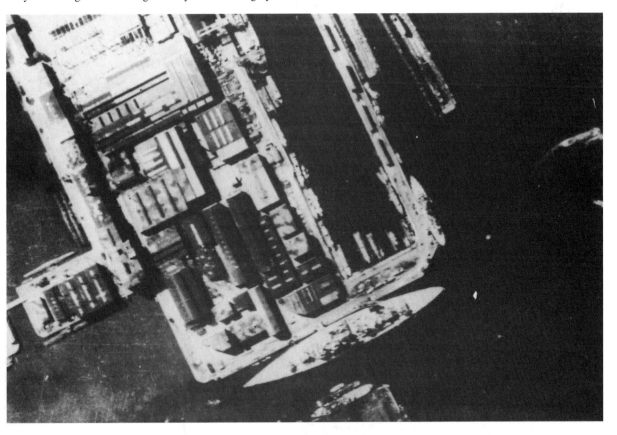

Above: Even in Gdynia it was still not possible for a ship to escape the attentions of the RAF. This photograph, taken by a British long-range reconnaissance aircraft, shows *Tirpitz* at Gdynia alongside the pier. At the top of the photograph, right of centre, are two floating docks, one of which is occupied, and in the inner basin are numerous ships and smaller craft. In the pool at left are three U-boats.

Above: On 5 May 1941 Hitler paid a surprise visit to Gdynia to inspect his two new battleships, *Bismarck*, anchored in the roadstead, and *Tirpitz*, in harbour at the pier. The photograph shows him leaving *Tirpitz*: on the upper deck the guard of honour, which includes a drummer and bugler, presents arms while the officers give the German salute.

Above: The Fleet Commander, *Admiral* Lütjens, and to his right his Chief of Staff, *Kapitän zur See* Netzbandt, take their leave of Hitler. It is noteworthy that this high-level visit took place in the absence of the Commander-in-Chief of the Navy, *Grossadmiral* Raeder. Lütjens and all his staff officers were to find a sailor's grave when *Bismarck* was sent to the bottom only three weeks later.

Right: *Tirpitz*'s captain, *Kapitän zur See* Topp, with his Executive Officer, *Fregattenkapitän* Paul Friedrich Düwel (right).

Above: Working-up in the Baltic. Here *Tirpitz* engages in gunnery practice in the autumn of 1941, firing a full salvo from all four barrels of her forward main turrets.

Above: A close-up taken at about the same time as the previous photograph, showing 'C' turret firing.

Above: Autumn 1941 in the Baltic. This stern view of *Tirpitz*, taken through a telephoto lens, gives an idea of her imposing size.

Above: A view from the bridge over the bows. 'A' turret is traversed to starboard. Notice the 2cm flak gun on the bridge platform below and the armoured command centre. The turntable mounting the 7m rangefinder and FuMO 23 radar antenna is also facing to starboard.

Above: Gun cleaning after firing practice, in this case the right barrel of 'B' turret. The size of the gang required for the task gives an idea of the heavy work involved.

Above: A muzzle view into one of the 38cm barrels of 'D' turret, clearly showing the rifling which imparts spin to the shells.

Left: A view over the bow showing 'A' turret—this was never fitted with the 10.5cm base stereoescopic range-finder—traversed to starboard, while 'B' turret is trained to port.

Below left: A meeting with a Type II coastal U-boat. A 10.5cm flak twin mounting and the port-side crane can clearly be seen; behind the crane can be seen one arm of the 6.5m rangefinder protruding through the PII 15cm turret.

Right: A 1942 photograph of the bridge/funnel complex. On the foretop there is now an additional observation position on the revolving platform and, supplementing the FuMO 23, a mattress aerial for FuMO 27 (here facing to port). On the superstructure deck are two twin 10.5cm flak mountings, each to the left of a 15cm gun turret; the 15cm turret on the left hand side is fitted with a 6.5m rangefinder. The revolving dome of the control centre carrying the FuMO 23 aerial bears to starboard; the crane is in the immobilised position; and two ship's boats are lashed down and covered. On the catapult abaft the funnel is an Arado 196 floatplane; and searchlights can be seen on the funnel platform.

Right: Training in the Baltic, 1941, with a Type VIIC U-boat alongside. Despite the major difference in size, the smallest submarine could be a very dangerous opponent even for a colossus like *Tirpitz*.

Above: A view astern from the foretop. Behind the funnel in the foreground is the pole mainmast, and beyond can be seen the aft flak control centre. The starboard crane is rigged towards the stern; and the main 'C' and 'D' turrets are trained to starboard and port respectively. Also visible on the port side are a 10.5cm twin flak mounting and PIII 15cm turret.

Above: September 1941 in the Baltic, with units of the so-called 'Baltic Fleet' on the move: (left to right) the battleship *Tirpitz*, in her wake the heavy cruiser *Admiral Scheer*, the light cruisers *Köln* and *Nürnberg* and the destroyers *Z27* and *Z26*. The photograph was taken from aboard the destroyer *Z25*.

Left: In January 1942 *Tirpitz* made a westward transit of the Kiel Canal and anchored in the roadstead off Wilhelmshaven prior to sailing for Norway. This photograph shows her during her transit of the canal.

Below: *Tirpitz* receives assistance from tugs during her journey through the Kiel Canal.

Above: *Tirpitz* in Norway, at Faettenfjord near Trondheim in February 1942. Alongside there are a number of supply vessels: the largest of these is probably a repair ship.

Above: Camouflage is everything. This scene shows *Tirpitz*'s bows, with 'A' and 'B' turrets draped with nets and the forecastle disguised as a woodland landscape of fir trees.

Above: The Faettenfjord anchorage seen from a nearby hillside. The ship is protected by a net barrage. It was not difficult for the numerous spies in the region to keep an eye on the battleship from either bank of the fjord, and enemy intelligence was always kept well informed of what went on.

Above: *Tirpitz* running in Lofoten waters. After the abandonment of Operation *'Sportpalast'*, the ship returned to anchor in Ofotfjord/ Westfjord unscathed, avoiding a number of attacks by British torpedo aircraft.

Right: *Tirpitz* at high speed, manouevring with her rudder hard over to avoid torpedoes dropped by aircraft. The tracks of two torpedoes are distinctly visible crossing the wake, to the right and left of the mast.

Below: A March 1942 photograph looking beyond the forward breakwaters and anchor capstans towards the Lofoten mountain chain in the distance.

Above: *Tirpitz* back in Faettenfjord. This photograph of the ship was taken between April and June 1942. During this period quadruple 2cm flak quadruples mountings were added on 'B' turret and on the bridge structure.

Left: The Commander-in-Chief of the *Kriegsmarine*, *Grossadmiral* Raeder, inspects *Tirpitz*. In his entourage are the Fleet Commander, *Admiral* Schniewind (immediately behind him), and to the latter's left *Vizeadmiral* Kummetz. At Raeder's right shoulder is *Kapitän zur See* Topp, *Tirpitz*'s commander.

Above: *Tirpitz* in Faettenfjord in the early summer of 1942. The net boom has been opened. The two newly installed quadruple 2cm flak mountings can be discerned in this photograph.

Above: Operation *'Rösselsprung'* (Knight's Move) in July 1942. German units having assembled in Altafjord preparatory to an offensive against the Allied Murmansk convoys, one of the two battle groups sets out, with *Tirpitz* leading the heavy cruisers *Admiral Hipper* and *Admiral Scheer*.

Above: The battle groups gather. To the left, dazzle painted, is the heavy cruiser *Admiral Hipper* and to the right *Tirpitz*. In the foreground are two destroyers.

Right: The battle groups sortie, 4 July 1942: a photograph taken from the battleship, showing the heavy cruiser *Admiral Hipper* leading *Tirpitz*.

Above: In this view of the battle groups taken from *Tirpitz*, the battleship is followed by the torpedo boats *T7* and *T15* and the heavy cruiser *Admiral Hipper*.

Above: A change in formation: the destroyer *Z25*, a torpedo boat and a second destroyer pass astern of *Tirpitz* in order to take up fresh stations within the squadron.

Above and below: These two images of *Tirpitz* in Altafjord were taken within a short time of each other and demonstrate the fickle weather conditions in high northern latitudes, a factor which hampered the operations of British bomber aircraft.

Above: *Tirpitz* in Altafjord, July 1942.

Above: Altafjord, December 1942: a view from the bow towards the bridge structure and the two forward 38cm turrets. Notice the two-colour scheme for the turret faces.

Above: A 1942 photograph of *Tirpitz* inside her net barrage in Kaafjord.

Right, top and centre: 1 February 1943: the departure of the ship's first commander, *Kapitän zur See* Topp, promoted to *Konteradmiral* effective that day. Here, already wearing his new uniform, Topp inspects the front rank of the ship's company.

Right: The visit of the Commander Naval Group Command North, *Generaladmiral* Karls, accompanied by the Fleet Commander, *Admiral* Schniewind, and the Senior Shipyard Director of the *Kriegsmarine* Yard, Trondheim, *Vizeadmiral* Eichel, March 1942.

Above: *Tirpitz* within her complex of anti-torpedo nets in Kaafjord.

Above and below: Two views of *Tirpitz* in Bogen Bay near Narvik in 1943, dwarfed by the surrounding mountains.

Above: September 1943: Operation *'Sizilien'*, the deployment of a powerful German naval force against Spitzbergen. The burning Barentsburg is seen from *Tirpitz*'s foredeck.

Above: 38cm shell cases on the upper deck. As distinct from Royal Navy practice, where cordite was always used in silk bags, the German Navy preferred metal cartridges.

Above: An inspection by *Admiral* Kummetz after the operation.

Right: In September 1943 the Royal Navy succeeded in severely damaging *Tirpitz* by the use of midget submarines. The photograph shows an X-craft of this type.

125

Above: *Tirpitz* in Kaafjord in the winter of 1943–44. From this photograph it can be appreciated how effectively camouflage paint blurs the contours of a ship.

Above: *Tirpitz* between May and August 1944 with a changed paint scheme. Notice the *Würzburg* radar system, installed on a raised platform around the after command position.

Above: A shipboard Arado 196 floatplane prepares for catapult launch.

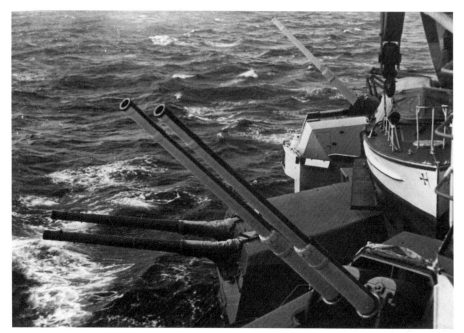

Left: Two twin 10.5cm flak guns and SII 15cm turret. The bow of the pinnace is emblazoned with an admiral's pennant, indicating that the boat is reserved for officers of that rank. In comparison with the photograph appearing earlier and taken from the same position in 1941, it is evident that the guns are now being included in camouflage schemes.

Above left: This aspect of the bridge complex, seen from the port quarter, provides a good view of the two stern-facing foretop turntables equipped with the 10.5cm rangefinder and FuMO 23 and FuMO 27 radar systems, and also the two forward flak fire control centres.

Above right: An exposure taken against the sun, looking towards the stem over the two quadruple 2cm flak mountings and 'A' and 'B' main turrets.

Left: Parade on the forecastle by division. Presumably there is no danger from aircraft as the two quadruple 2cm flak guns are covered. The crew of a warship is composed of divisions, the numbers and strength of which are related to the size of the ship. On smaller units up to destroyer size, there were usually only three divisions, but more on larger vessels. Tirpitz had twelve, each consisting of from 180 to 220 men arranged as follows: Divisions 1 to 4—seaman branch including personnel for the main and secondary armament; Divisions 5 and 6—seaman branch including flak personnel; Division 7—functionaries such as stewards, writers, cooks, cobblers and tailors; Division 8—artillery mechanical personnel; Division 9—navigation and signals; Divisions 10 to 12—ship's technicians. The divisions were split down into watches, starboard 1, 3 and 5 and port 2, 4 and 6, distinguished by coloured stripes sewn on the upper arm of the uniform.

Above: A photograph taken in 1944 from the forepeak towards 'A' and 'B' turrets. 'B' turret is trained to starboard, as is the FuMO 23 radar of the conning tower. The new FuMO 26 at the foretop is facing to port.

Left: One of the two quadruple 2cm flak mountings. As time went on, many more of these would need to be installed.

Above: A mixed group of officers, warrant officers, petty officers and ratings pose for the camera in summer 1941, with *Tirpitz* alongside the pier as a background.

Right: Morning parade on the forecastle: the most senior petty officer of a division reports the men of his watch to the Divisional Officer.

Above: Norway, spring 1942: a group photograph taken forward of 'A' and 'B' turrets.

Above: Norway, spring 1942: an assembly of the full 8th Division.

Right: Looking aft from the starboard superstructure deck: a view of the ship's company parading on the quarterdeck. This photograph was probably taken in the autumn of 1942.

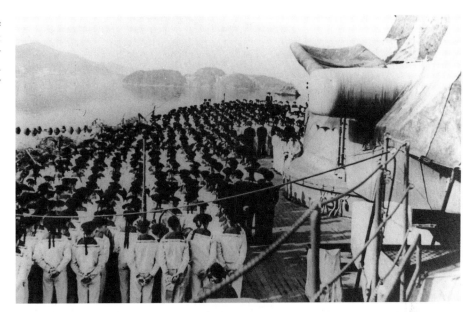

Right, centre and bottom: Two photographs of the warrant officers' mess, Christmas 1942.

Above: *Tirpitz* in 1944. The new large FuMO 26 radar aerial can be seen on the control tower. Repairs are presumably being carried out to earlier damage. Notice the swastika air recognition symbol painted on the foredeck.

Above: The ship's corps of warrant officers: an autumn 1941 photograph.

Right: A look into the warrant officers' mess. The photograph gives only a partial view of the mess but still manages to convey the impression of how busy it was at mealtimes when the ship was in harbour or otherwise inactive. While at sea, a portion of the mess membership would be on watch, and meals would then be taken in shifts.

Above and right: Two photographs of the ship's interior, here the electrical switchrooms—an apparent confusion of handwheels and instruments.

Above: One of the numerous flak positions sited on the mountainsides and promontories surrounding the ship's anchorage. Here an installation receives a visit from crew members during a ramble.

Left: A warrant officer's cabin, in this case that of *E-Stabsobermaschinst* (Senior Electrical ERA) Schmolke.

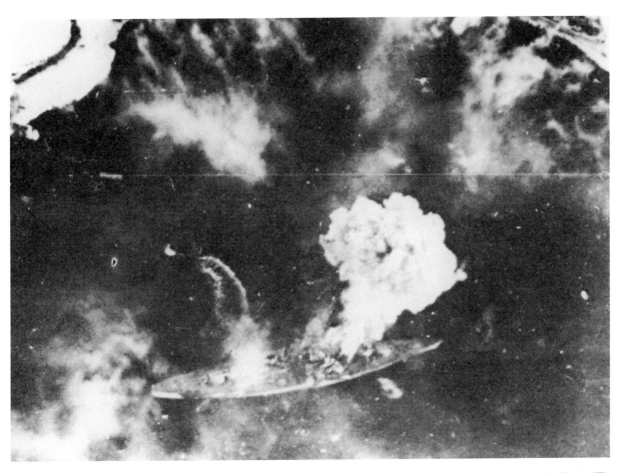

Above: The attack of 3 April 1944 sounded the death knell for *Tirpitz*. This British aerial photograph shows the ship lying in Altafjord amid a hail of bombs, her attempted smoke-screen not yet having been fully deployed.

Right: A photograph taken on 15 April showing the damage caused on the 3rd. Burnt-out rooms and a splinter-riddled superstructure are evident.

Above: A photograph showing the severity of the damage.

Left: One of the 10.5cm flak guns knocked out by blast.

138

Right: Looking down on the port superstructure deck: at top right is the damaged twin 10.5cm flak gun, at bottom right the damaged crane. The deck is strewn with wreckage.

Below: Another view over the port quarter, where the funnel mantle and upperworks have obvious fire damage. The flak guns are all unserviceable.

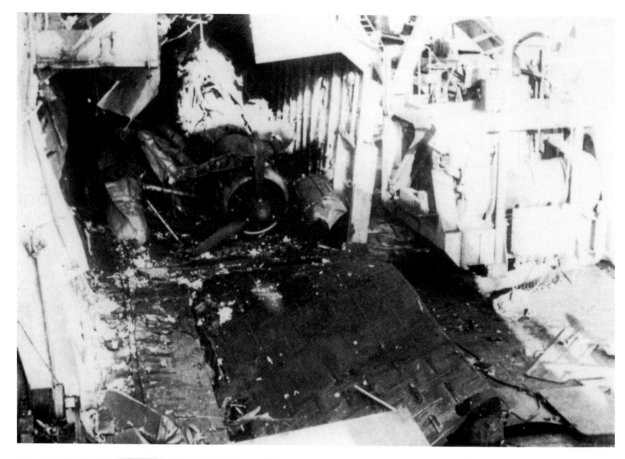

Above: A burnt-out aircraft in the ruins of its hangar.

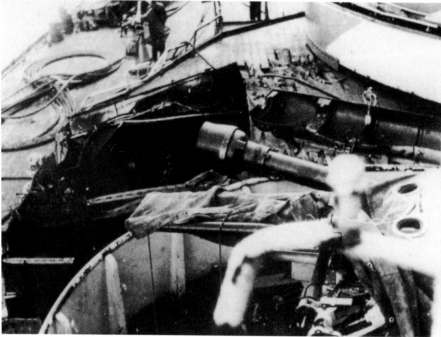

Left: Heavy damage to the port-side superstructure forward at bridge deck level.

140

Right: Damaged bulkheads on the superstructure deck.

Below: The burial service for the crew members killed during the attack of 3 April 1944. Losses were particularly heavy amongst the flak gunners.

Above and left: The funeral ceremony for the ship's dead.

Above: *Tirpitz* inside her net defences at Kaafjord on 2 June 1944.

Above: This photograph, taken over Kaafjord at 0630hrs, shows *Tirpitz* making smoke following receipt of an air raid warning.

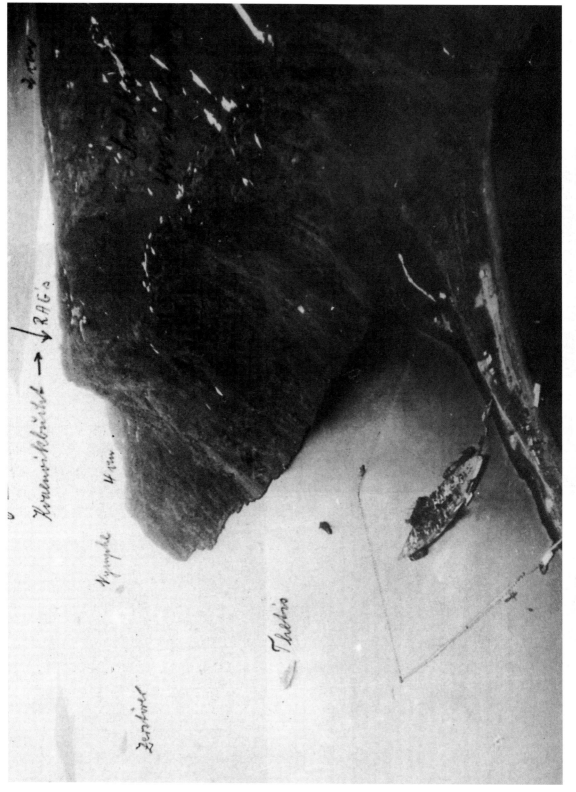

Above: *Tirpitz* at Kaafjord. The flak ships *Nymphe* and *Thetis* are moored close by to provide additional protection whilst numerous 4cm and 2cm flak guns and other AA systems have been installed on the surrounding mountainsides.

Above: An exposure taken on 30 June 1944 above the anchorage at Kaafjord.

Above: This British reconnaissance photograph, taken after a further heavy attack, shows *Tirpitz* at the centre of several large oil slicks which indicate leaks. The starboard crane was destroyed in the attack, and the battleship has numerous auxiliary craft and lighters alongside. Repair work is already well under way.

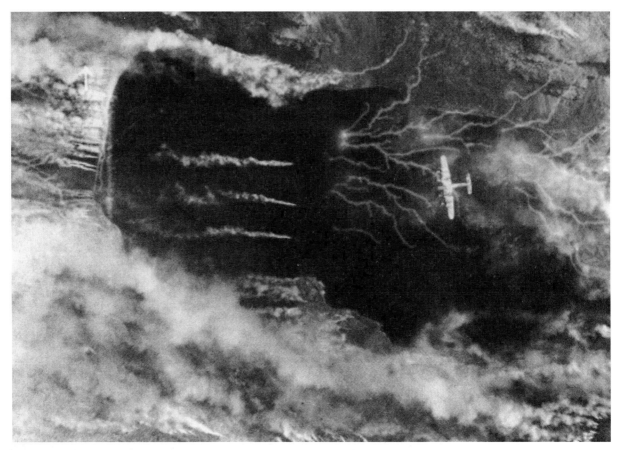

Above: A British aerial photograph dated 15 September 1944. The effort to cover the area in smoke is self-evident. One of the attacking four-engine bombers is at the centre of the picture.

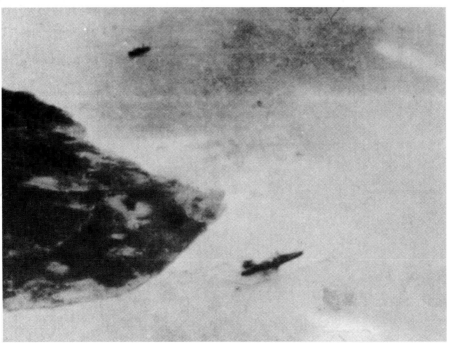

Left: The end: 12 November 1944. From long range *Tirpitz* attempts to put up a shrapnel barrage with her main 38cm armament.

146

Right: *Tirpitz* shrouded by gigantic fountains of water from near misses and the billowing smoke of direct hits; note, left, the explosive cloud from a wide miss. All hope for the ship is now gone.

Right: The bright point at the foot of the cloud of smoke is the explosion of a direct hit. Both this and the previous photograph were taken from an altitude of about 2,000m

Right: The bright pinpoint in the murk denotes another direct hit. This photograph was taken from about 4,000m.

Left: As the ship is devastated by fire, another bomb explodes well wide of the target.

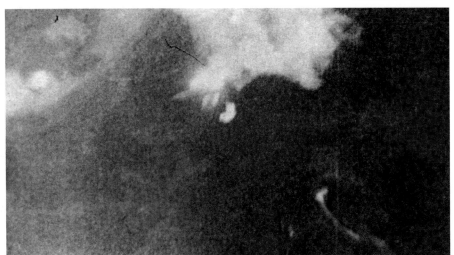

Left: A huge cloud of smoke blankets the ship.

Left: The end: *Tirpitz* in her death throes.

Right: The ship capsizes.

Right: Shortly afterwards, rescue teams board the upturned hull to save what they can. Among them are many of the ship's technical specialists, most importantly the pump masters. Thanks to their knowledge of the state of the ship, its divisions and the warren of compartments, they succeeded eventually in extricating more than 80 members of the ship's company entombed in the hull.

Right: The repair vessel *Huascaran* goes alongside.

149

Above: Work starts on breaking *Tirpitz* up, 22 March 1949.

Conclusions

In the years following the Second World War, more so once it became possible to study the documents and files returned to the German archives by the victorious powers, many books were published about the war at sea, including the history of operations by battle groups or independent warships—often factual accounts of a popular type—together with articles in technical journals. German naval construction in particular was placed under the microscope for detailed criticism. Although many of the opinions rendered were subjective, it is true to say that the overwhelming majority of publications tried to be objective.

A Memorandum issued by the VDI (*Verein Deutscher Ingenieure* = Society of German Engineers) and drawn up by eminent former naval technical experts, came generally to the following conclusions:

'What the *Kriegsmarine* lacked in the naval building programme between 1933 and 1938 was not the means but proper planning. The circle responsible for the *Kriegsmarine* as it was at the outbreak of war in 1939 had failed to understand the nature of what they were supposed to be doing, and for this reason:

'Warships above destroyer size were supposed to be built for ocean raiding in the Atlantic. Away from German home ports, a ship can only effectively prosecute warfare against commerce if she has endurance. This factor was taken into account by the designers of the *Deutschland* class *Panzerschiffe*, which were diesel-powered. All the less comprehensible, therefore, was the departure from this path in 1934 and the return to steam propulsion as seen in *Scharnhorst* and *Gneisenau* and later in *Bismarck* and *Tirpitz*. There was, especially for Germany, hardly a less suitable type than the *Admiral Hipper* class heavy cruiser with its inadequate armament (20.3cm), inadequate armour and miserable endurance. They were as useless as they were superfluous.'

Hull and Armour Protection

With the exception of Germany, all sea powers used the 'all or nothing' protection system for modern capital ships, while the designers of the *Bismarck* and *Tirpitz* based their plans on the Imperial Navy's final development of the genre, *Baden* and *Bayern*, whose protection had been an improved version of that of their predecessors which saw combat at Jutland in 1916. In the time since the *Bayern* class, German capital ship contruction had been in an impasse: no experience had been gained, and no test and experimental facilities set up. Defeat in 1918 had brought about the forfeiture of all modern capital ships, and—except for a minimal force for coast defence—whatever else Germany was left with had had to be surrendered or scrapped. Possibilities considered as test-beds were the two remote-controlled target ships, *Hessen* and *Zähringen*, found to be unavailable for experimental purposes, and also the old coal hulk *Falk* and the midships section of the scrapped pre-dreadnought *Preussen* (the last available only for underwater explosives testing). Not a single surplus ship existed for extensive experimentation.

Apart from the generally more modern equipment, what distinguished *Bismarck* from *Baden* was greater dimensions and better quality armour. The increased output of the former's machinery by 250 per cent, from the 52,800shp of the *Baden* to 138,000shp, was accompanied by an increase in top speed from 22.5 to 30kts. The larger engine plant required more space, resulting in a lengthening of the hull and a broader beam of 36m. The latter endowed the hull with high initial stability, which made *Bismarck* a reliable gun platform. Another important feature was the compartmentalisation of the hull, created by a system of transverse and longitudinal bulkheads.

The belt armour was designed to withstand, under normal circumstances, the impact of a 38cm shell fired from a range of 15.5km at right angles. That was the theory, but in practice the angle would be finer and the effective strength of the armour correspondingly greater. The German Navy always preferred the vertical arrangement of the main belt armour and an effective and comprehensive division of the armour protection above the hull in contrast to the 'raft body' (compact citadel) principle preferred by the United States and France.

Until about 1930, naval constructors clung to the old rule of thumb that the thickness of the belt armour should correspond to the calibre of the main battery. Weapons experts eventually came to the conclusion that in the eternal battle between armour and shell, the shell would finally win, and as a consequence the rule fell into disuse for belt armour, the new determining factors for armour strength and the extent of the belt being the ship's displacement and compartmentalisation. The greater ranges obtained following the introduction of new fire control systems was also a contributory factor, but the corollary of 'plunging fire'—the arrival of a shell at an angle less than 20 degrees from the vertical—introduced a problem that had to be resolved, requiring as it did the strengthening of the horizontal armour, and this protection aboard German heavy units proved inadequate. The matter did not become apparent until after the outbreak of war in 1939, for not until then was the danger of air attack fully appreciated. *Bismarck* was the example which clearly demonstrated that units of this size without air cover and proceeding independently were highly vulnerable to air attack. The same lesson was driven home to the British a little later when HMS *Repulse* and *Prince of Wales* were sunk by Japanese bombers. The capital ship, which until then had dominated naval doctrine by virtue of its fire power alone, now needed adequate armour and in addition the protection of an escort force in order to operate, and this role was taken over by the fast aircraft carrier.

The guided bomb and aerial torpedo gained increasingly in significance. The angle of impact of the bomb was almost vertical, and a 500kg bomb dropped from 4,500m could easily punch through 152mm armour plate. In contrast to their overseas counterparts, German heavy units never managed to cope with the danger from the air: both *Tirpitz* and *Bismarck*, not to mention the other big ships, gave a poor account of themselves in this respect.

The horizontal armour was their great weakness. In July 1941, at La Pallice, *Scharnhorst* was hit by a 1,000lb bomb which went straight through 191mm armour plate. Of five hits on the starboard side, two penetrated the upper armour deck, the battery deck and 'tween deck and exploded in the lower armour deck. The other three also went through all decks.

Other than the fact that the quality of the armour had been substantially improved, the single advance in the *Bismarck* class over the *Bayern* class was an additional armour deck near the waterline, horizontal above the magazines and the propulsion machinery and sloping down to the underside of the armour belt at an angle of 25 degrees.

The upper deck of the *Tirpitz* could withstand a plunging 6in (15.2cm) shell but not a 500lb semi-armour piercing bomb dropped from 900m. Therefore the whole volume of the ship above the waterline—with the exception of the turrets and barbettes—was vulnerable to bombs and shells. This constructional weakness is highlighted in the case of the *Bismarck* and *Tirpitz*: during her final battle with the British capital ships *Rodney* and *King George V*, *Bismarck* received most of the hits from 16in and 14in shells at short range, but not at an angle threatening the main armour deck. There were a few hits at the start of the action which caused heavy casualties amongst *Bismarck*'s command officers, in the fire control centres and particularly in the command relay centres. As the battle reached its concluding phase, *Bismarck* was shot to pieces from stem to stern above the waterline, and three torpedoes more would have been enough to sink her: the fact that she was scuttled by opening the seacocks and detonating explosive charges before that point was reached should not obscure the reality.

Three years later *Tirpitz* was hit by a number of bombs, none of which exploded below the armour deck although the installations above it were destroyed. She suffered heavy losses in personnel. Only five bombs exploded below the upper deck.

Machinery

The return to steam propulsion for *Bismarck* and *Tirpitz* was a direct result of the haste with which the

German Navy rearmed. The experience derived from the high-compression steam installations aboard the fleet escorts *F1* to *F10* and the state yacht *Grille*, and also in the early destroyers, ought really to have convinced the naval planners to take the more difficult path of designing an effective diesel. The goodwill of the manufacturers must surely have been on hand, the diesel motor had many advocates within naval circles, and the installations aboard the three armoured ships had been fully proved. However, there was a ruling clique in the *Kriegsmarine* which preferred to plod along a well-worn track and its view prevailed.

The German Navy was unique amongst the naval powers in preferring the three-shaft drive for its capital ships, an installation obviously lighter by far than the four-shaft drive of foreign heavy ships and one which acquitted itself very satisfactorily.

The unlucky torpedo hit on the *Bismarck*'s rudder was a rare stroke of misfortune and is irrelevant to any assessment.

Weapons and Fire Control Systems

The designers of the *Bismarck* class adhered to the tried and tested main armament arrangement of two twin turrets forward and aft, the rearmost of each superfiring. The reason for this was the better field of fire and more effective sequence of salvos. The smaller calibres—the 15cm secondary artillery and the 10.5cm flak—followed the previous layout.

The concept of the 15cm gun was its role as a classic anti-destroyer weapon. It fired a theoretical eight, but in practice only six, rounds per barrel per minute, and was in no respects of any value as an anti-aircraft gun, having too slow a rate of fire and turret rotation speed and an inadequate angle of elevation. Together with the main armament, it was used on *Tirpitz* in an anti-aircraft role as it could put up a long-range barrage of time-fused shells to confront approaching bomber formations with a curtain of shrapnel.

German naval flak was inadequate, and lacked a gun which was capable of engaging both a fast bomber at high altitude and long distance and also a torpedo bomber closing in just above the wave tops. The planners had failed to grasp the concept of the multi-purpose flak gun. There would certainly have been room for them, but it was left to other navies to address the

problem and to come up with workable solutions towards the end of the war. Of course, Germany already had an excellent flak gun, the 12.7cm Flak L/45 Model 34, which had a range, at 30 degrees' elevation, of 10,497.3m, a shell weight of 23.45kg and a muzzle velocity of 829.97m/sec and which had given outstanding results against enemy bombers over the Reich.

The VDI-Memorandum (which had had handwritten comments added in April 1957 by former ministerial adviser *Dipl-Ing* Ludwig Cordes, from December 1942 Chief of the Official Group for Artillery Construction at Naval Command, a personality familiar with the whole subject inside and out) drew special attention to fire direction centres with the following notable conclusion:

'There was no technical expert at Naval Command (OKM) charged with responsibility for this particular interest. Rulings were ultimately within the jurisdiction of a military centre, which led to frequent erroneous decisions.'

Flak

There were two different models. The 10.5cm model C33 guns of *Bismarck* were fitted in twin mountings, C31 forward and C37 aft. The guns differed principally in the coordination system for their target data. In themselves both weapons were flawless, but unfortunately when the C37 had been shipped, the necessity to install the fire direction equipment individual to each model of gun had been overlooked, with the result that, when the fire direction instructions were transmitted, Flak C33 fired at the target and Flak C37 at a point beyond it. The error here clearly lay with *Kriegsmarine* planning, which resulted in the linking of an incompatible battery to the control centre.

Flak Direction Centres

Until the end of the war, German heavy units were equipped with grossly inferior flak direction centres based on the Cardan ring system with a large revolving base. At a massive 40 tons, their weight tended to affect the ship's stability. In battle, many defects came to light, for the Cardan ring system was very sensitive to underwater hits: even the lightest hits could cause a break in the ring, resulting in a total system breakdown.

As early as 1932 engineers had set out proposals for an improved and more suitable development which had a smaller and triaxial rotating base. Despite repeated reminders, it was not until 1942 that the new device was first commissioned, and the experimental prototype was eventually ready by the end of the war though never fitted aboard ship. Complementing a far superior handling capability and better armour protection, the new device had a weight of only 6 tons.

In 1933 proposals had been put forward for automatic fire direction mountings for 3.7cm and 2cm guns. This demonstrates how far-sighted the German weapons engineering industry was, but in this case nothing came of the proposals.

Radar Equipment

At the outbreak of war in 1939 Germany had two workable radar systems, *Freya* (2.4cm waveband) and *Würzburg* (50cm waveband). At the time, the Third Reich led the world in this field. This would change. In the autumn of that year the British built a 12m system and then concentrated their efforts on the centimetre wavebands. In 1943, they introduced the 9cm device known to the Germans as 'Rotterdam'.

In Germany the industry was fragmented, and instead of drawing on the experience of well-established firms, new companies were set up and the *Luftwaffe* commandeered all new developments. In 1942–43 it was decided that no new developments in radars of wavebands less than 20cm were possible, and all research into that area was abandoned. Only when a 'Rotterdam' set fell into German hands was work resumed. None of the equipment built worked satisfactorily in service. Germany had 'missed the bus'.

These few concluding remarks may be sufficient to permit a more critical assessment of German warship construction of the period than is normally the case. At their completion, the two *Bismarck* class units were the culmination of capital ship building, but they were already obsolescent. They were powerful and sturdy fighting ships, but not unsinkable. In their final form they were, asthetically, the crowning glory of German warship construction.

The destruction by *Bismarck* of the world's largest capital ship of the time, the battlecruiser *Hood*, is an impressive testimonial to German naval gunnery. But in respect of this success, it must be remembered that it was achieved against a warship which had been laid down in the Great War twenty-five years previously—certainly modernised but unchanged in her basic structure.

Bibliography

Books

Assmann, Kurt, *Deutsche Seestrategie in zwei Weltkriegen*, Heidelberg, 1957

Baum, Walter, and Weichhold, Eberhard, *Der Krieg der 'Achsenmächte' im Mittelmeerraum*, Göttingen, 1973

Bennett, Geoffrey, *Seeschachten im 2. Weltkrieg*, Koblenz/Bonn, 1981

Bidlingmaier, Gerhard, *Einsatz der schweren Kriegsmarineeinheiten im ozeanischen Zufuhrkrieg*, Nechargemünd, 1969

Bismarck, Otto Fürst von, *Gedanken und Erinnerungen*, 3 vols, Stuttgart/Berlin, 1905

Bräckow, Werner, *Die Geschichte der deutschen Marine-Ingenieur-Offizierskorps*, Oldenburg, 1974

Brennecke, Jochen, *Schlachtschiff Bismarck*, Herford, 1960

———, *Schlachtschiff Tirpitz*, Herford, 1978

Breyer, Siegfried, *Schlachtschiffe und Schlachtkreuzer 1905–1970*, München, 1970

———, *Grosskampfschiffe 1905–1970. Bd 1: Grossbritannien und Deutschland*, München, 1977

Breyer, Siegfried, and Koop, Gerhard, *Von der Emden zur Tirpitz*, München, 1982

———, *Die deutsche Kriegsmarine. Bd 4 und 5*, Friedburg, 1988/89

Brown, David, *Die Tirpitz*, München, 1980

Chesneau, Roger, (ed.), *Conway's All the World's Fighting Ships 1922–1946*, London, 1980

Churchill, Winston S., *Der Zweite Weltkrieg. Erster Bd*, Bern, 1949

Diwald, Helmut, *Der Kampf um die Weltmeere*, München/Zürich, 1980

Dönitz, Karl, *Zehn Jahre und zwanzig Tage. Erinnerungen 1939–1945*, Koblenz, 1985

Dülffer, Jost, *Weimar, Hitler und die Marine*, Düsseldorf, 1972

Dulin and Garzke, *Battleships*, Vol. 3, Annapolis, 1986

Engelberg, Ernst, *Bismarck: Urpreusse und Reichsgründer*, Berlin, 1985

Evers, *Kriegsschiffbau*, Berlin, 1943

Friedman, Norman, *Battleships*, London, 1978

Gall, Lothar, *Bismarck: der weisse Revolutionär*, Frankfurt a. M., 1980

Grenfell, Russell, *Jagd auf die Bismarck*, Tübingen, 1958

Gröner, Erich, *Die deutschen Kriegsschiffe 1815–1945. Bd 1 und 2*, Koblenz, 1989

Haffner, Sebastian, *Von Bismarck zu Hitler*, München, 1981

Haffner, Sebastain/Venohr, Wolfgang, *Preussische Profile*, Frankfurt a. M./Berlin, 1986

Handbuch zur deutschen Militärgeschichte 1648–1939. Hrsg. vom Militärgeschichtlichen Forschungsamt. Bd 4/Abschnitt VIII: Deutsche Marinegeschichte der Neuzeit, München, 1979

Hildebrand, Hans H.; Stöhr, Albert; and Steinmetz, Hans-Otto, *Die deutschen Kriegsschiffe. Biographien. Bd 1 und 6*, Herford, 1979 and 1982

Irving, David, *Die Schlacht im Eismeer: Der Untergang des Geleitzuges PQ 17*, Hamburg, 1982

Lewin, Ronald, *Entschied Ultra den Krieg? Alliierte Funkaufklärung im 2. Weltkrieg*, Koblenz/Bonn, 1981

Lohmann, Walter, and Hildebrand, Hans H., *Die deutsche Kriegsmarine 1939–1945: Gliederung, Organisation, Stellenbesetzung*, 3 vols, Bad Nauheim, 1956–1964

MacLean, Alistair, *Die Männer der Ulysses*, Berlin, 1957

Müllenheim-Rechberg, Burkhard Frhr von, *Schlachtschiff Bismarck 1940/41*, Berlin, 1980

Peillard, Leonce, *Versenkt die Tirpitz!*, Wiesbaden, 1977

Pemsel, Helmut, *Seeherrschaft: Eine maritime Weltgeschichte von den Anfängen der Seefahrt bis zur Gegenwart*, 2 vols, Koblenz, 1985

———, *Biographisches Lexikon zur Seekriegsgeschichte*, Koblenz, 1985

Potter, Elmer B.; Nimitz, Chester W.; and Rohwer, Jürgen, *Seemacht: Eine Seekriegsgeschichte von der Antike bis zur Gegenwart*, München, 1974

Raeder, Erich, *Mein Leben*, 2 vols, Tübingen, 1956/57

Raven, Alan, and Roberts, John, *Die britischen Schlachtschiffe des Zweiten Weltkrieges*, 3 vols, München, 1980/81

Rohwer, Jürgen, and Hümmelchen, Gerhard, *Chronik des Seekrieges 1939–1945*, Oldenburg/Hamburg, 1968

Rössle, Wilhelm, *Bismarcks Politik nach seinen Staatsschriften und Reden*, Jena, 1943

Rothfels, Hans, *Bismarck und der Staat*, Stuttgart, 1964

Salewski, Michael, *Die deutsche Seekriegsleitung 1935–1945*, 3 vols, Frankfurt a.M./München, 1970–1975

———, *Tirpitz: Aufstieg, Macht, Scheitern*, Göttingen, 1979

Santoni, Alberto, *Ultra siegt im Mittelmeer: Die entscheidende Rolle der britischen Funkaufklärung 1940–1943*, Koblenz, 1985

Schmalenbach, Paul, *Die Geschichte der deutschen Schiffsartillerie*, Herford, 1968

Schofield, Brian, *Der Untergang der Bismarck*, Stuttgart, 1976

Tirpitz, Alfred von, *Erinnerungen*, Leipzig, 1919

———, *Politische Dokumente: Deutsche Ohnmachtspolitik im Weltkriege*, Hamburg/Berlin, 1926

Wagner, Gerhard, (ed.), *Lagevorträge des Oberbefehlshabers der Kriegsmarine vor Hitler 1939–1945*, München, 1972

Periodicals

Jahrbuch der Schiffbautechnischen Gesellschaft (various years)

Marinearsenal (various issues)

Marineforum (various years)

Marine Rundschau (various years)

Schiffbau (various years)

Daily and weekly newspapers and magazines (various editions)

Sources

Bundesarchiv/Militärarchiv, Freiburg im Breisgau (plans)

Koop archive

Public Record Office: 'Tirpitz: an account of the various attacks carried out by the British Armed Forces and their effect upon the German Battleship', Vol. 2: Evidence for detailed accounts of damage, BR 1736(22)B.

Index of Ships

About the Authors

GERHARD KOOP

Gerhard Koop was born in 1926 and entered the *Kriegsmarine* in 1941 for pre-NCO training, followed by service in the U-boat arm. He was a member of the Federal Frontier Protection Force from 1951 but transferred to the Federal German Navy in 1956. From then until 1975 he served aboard motor torpedo boats, submarine-chasers, minesweepers, frigates and supply ships as ship's technical officer. During the period 1960–62 he lectured at a Naval Technical School. In 1975 he was appointed as a specialist in ships' motors at Naval Support Command. He retired in 1981.

His journalistic activities have involved him as author, technical translator and collaborator in naval/historical and naval/technical works. His publications are:

Die deutschen Segelschulschiffe (with K. P. Schmolke, 1989)

Planrolle: Segelschulschiff 'Gorch Fock' (II) (with K. P. Schmolke, 1989)

Die Marine in Wilhelmshaven (with E. Mulitze, 1987)

'Emden': Ein Name-fünf Schiffe (1983)

Von der Kaiserlichen Werft zum Marinearsenal (with K. Galle and F. Klein, 1982)

Von der 'Emden' zur 'Tirpitz' (with S. Breyer, 2 vols, 1981–82)

Die Schiffe und Fahrzeuge der deutschen Bundesmarine 1956-76 (with S. Breyer, 1978)

Translations

Kriegsschiffe der Welt 1860–1905 (3 vols, 1983–85)

Howard, *Segel-Kriegsschiffe 1400–1860* (1983)

Raven/Roberts, *Die britischen Schlachtschiffe des Zweiten Weltkrieges* (3 vols, 1980–81)

Brown, *Die 'Tirpitz'* (1980)

KLAUS-PETER SCHMOLKE

Klaus Peter-Schmolke is one of the finest draughtsmen of ships and scale drawings in Germany and has collaborated on a series of specialist publications, including *Die deutschen Segelschulschiffe*, 1989, and *Planrolle: Schulsegelschiff 'Gorch Fock'*, 1989, both with Gerhard Koop.